SELF-CONI

GUIDEBOOK FUR

TEENS

The Road To Self-Discovery, Overcoming
Self-Doubt, And Reaching Your Full
Potential

TEEN RISE

CONTENT

INTRODUCTION

Hey there, you. Yes, you, the teenager reading this book right now. Let's be real for a moment: being a teenager can be tough. You're going through all sorts of changes, both physical and emotional. You're trying to figure out who you are and where you fit in the world. And on top of all that, you're bombarded with messages from the media, your peers, and even your own inner voice telling you that you're not good enough. It's no wonder that confidence can be hard to come by when you're a teenager. But here's the thing: confidence is not some elusive quality that only a lucky few possess. It's not something that you either have or you don't. Rather, it's a skill that you can learn and develop, just like any other skill.

Think of it like a superpower. Just like a superhero learns to control and harness their powers, you can learn to control and harness your confidence. And just like a superhero, you have to put in the work to develop your superpower. It's not always easy, but it's worth it. In fact, confidence can be one of the most valuable skills you can have as a teenager. When you're confident, you're more likely to take risks, try new things, and speak up for yourself. You're less likely to be held back by fear and self-doubt. And as you move into adulthood, confidence can be a key factor in your success, both personally and professionally.

But how do you develop confidence? Unfortunately, there's no class or book that can make the confidence building process quick, easy, and painless. It's a process that takes time and effort. And it starts with understanding what confidence really means. Confidence is not about being perfect or never making mistakes. Believe me. I have self-confidence and I'm constantly messing up. It's also not about never feeling afraid or uncertain. That's just an unrealistic expectation for yourself. The thing is, at the heart of it, confidence is about believing in yourself and your abilities, even when things get tough. It's about trusting that you can handle whatever comes your way. And it's about being willing to take risks and learn from your failures.

I know it can seem intimidating and downright impossible to embark on a massive self-improvement journey at this point in your life, but that's where I come in. There are plenty of strategies and techniques you can use to improve your own self-confidence, many of which you will find in this book. As you read on, keep in mind that I'm not here to tell you what you should and shouldn't do - that isn't my desire or my place. I am here only to guide you as you explore yourself at your own pace, and in your own way.

That being said, I can also tell you that the most important thing you can do to begin this journey is to work on accepting yourself for who you are. You are unique, with your own strengths, weaknesses, and quirks. And that's okay. In fact, it's more than okay - it's what makes you who you are. When you accept yourself, flaws and all, you take the first step toward building confidence. You stop comparing yourself to others and start focusing on your own journey.

Of course, accepting yourself is easier said than done. It's hard not to feel self-conscious or insecure when you're surrounded by images of seemingly perfect people on social media or in the media. But remember, those images are often carefully curated and edited. They don't show the whole picture. It can also be hard to accept yourself when you're constantly receiving messages that you're not good enough. Maybe you've been bullied, or maybe you've just internalized negative messages from the world around you. Whatever the case, it's important to recognize that these messages are not true. You are good enough, just as you are.

A common first step on this self-acceptance venture is to focus on your strengths. What are you good at? What do you enjoy doing? What makes you unique? Make a list of your strengths and read it over when you're feeling down. Remember that everyone has weaknesses, but focusing on your strengths can help you feel more confident and capable. If you encounter moments of weakness or insecurity while working through this book, look back on this list and remind yourself of how amazing it is that you are so perfectly, imperfectly you.

Another thing we will discuss later is how to set goals for yourself. I don't blame you if your first thought was "I already know how to set goals, I'm not 5." The thing is, I didn't even learn how to set realistic goals until my junior year of college, when I took a class on time management and some other stereotypical success strategies. I was struggling with undiagnosed ADHD at the time, and I needed the wake up call that I was constantly setting myself up for failure and disappointment. I learned that having a clear idea of what you want to achieve can give you a sense of purpose and direction. Starting small isn't a sign of weakness or inability, it is a sign that you respect yourself enough to set yourself up for success. As you achieve these smaller goals, you'll start to build momentum and feel more confident taking on bigger challenges.

The thing is, I also learned that setting goals is only the first step. You also need to take action to achieve those goals. This can be scary, especially if you're afraid of failure. But remember, failure is not the end of the world. In fact, it's often the best way to learn and grow. When you're working toward a goal, it's important to have a growth mindset. This means that you believe that your abilities can be developed through hard work and dedication.

You understand that failure is a natural part of the learning process, and you use your failures as opportunities to learn and improve. That was a real doozy for me. I still catch myself with the negative self-talk and have to consciously turn it around.

One of the later concepts we will discuss is the importance of surrounding yourself with positive influences. This means seeking out people who support and encourage you, rather than tearing you down. It also means consuming media that uplifts and inspires you, rather than making you feel bad about yourself. I know the word is often overused, but purging the toxic people and behaviors from your life is like pulling weeds in a garden. It's hard work and you usually don't want to do it, but then you see how much better your garden grows with them gone and suddenly it's worth it.

As I am sure you've gathered from all of this, building confidence is a journey. With that in mind, it is important to remember that there will be setbacks and challenges along the way. But as long as you keep working at it, you will start to see progress, and before you know it, you'll be harnessing your superpower of confidence, ready to take on whatever the world throws your way. So, are you ready to start your journey to becoming a confident teenager? It won't always be easy, but I promise it will be worth it. Remember, you are capable of amazing things. You just have to believe in yourself.

1.

FROM SABOTEUR TO ALLY:

TRANSFORMING SELF-CRITICISM INTO SELF-LOVE

"The greatest discovery of my generation is that a human being can alter his life by altering his attitudes." - William James

If you're reading this, chances are you're struggling with negative thoughts and beliefs that are holding you back from reaching your full potential. You may be dealing with a constant inner voice telling you that you're not good enough or that you're destined to fail. Maybe you've even given up on pursuing your dreams because you don't believe in yourself. But here's the thing: those negative thoughts and beliefs are not the truth. They're just stories that you've been telling yourself for so long that you've started to believe them. But just like any story, they can be rewritten.

You have the power to challenge those negative thoughts and beliefs and replace them with positive ones. It's not an overnight process, but it's a journey that's worth taking. In fact, it's one of the most important journeys you can take as a teenager. Why? Because those negative thoughts and beliefs are holding you back from your full potential. They're like a heavy anchor that's keeping you from reaching your goals and living the life you truly want. But once you learn how to identify and confront those negative thoughts, you'll be amazed at how much lighter and freer you'll feel. You'll be able to take risks, try new things, and speak up for yourself without the constant fear and self-doubt holding you back.

So how do you start? It begins with understanding the impact that thoughts and beliefs have on your self-confidence. The way you think about yourself and your abilities directly affects how you feel and act. Negative thoughts and beliefs can make you feel small, powerless, and defeated. But positive thoughts and beliefs can make you feel strong, capable, and unstoppable. One way to start identifying the negative thoughts and beliefs that are weighing you down is through thought awareness exercises. By paying attention to your thoughts and how they make you feel, you can start to recognize certain patterns of negative thinking. Once you've identified them, you can start to challenge and replace them with more positive and empowering thoughts. This is the basis for something called cognitive behavioral therapy

(CBT), which is used commonly by psychologists to help rewire the brain for positive thinking.

It's important to understand some of the common thought patterns that lead to negative beliefs, such as all-or-nothing thinking and self-blame. By recognizing these patterns, you can learn to reframe your thoughts in a more positive light, which then helps teach your brain to default to positivity rather than negativity.

And of course, as plenty of self-help books will tell you, positive self-talk and visualization are powerful tools for building confidence. By speaking to yourself in a kind and supportive way, and visualizing yourself succeeding in your goals, you can start to build a foundation of self-belief that will carry you forward.

In this chapter, we'll dive deeper into the impact of negative thoughts and beliefs on your self-confidence, and we'll give you practical tools and exercises to start confronting those negative beliefs and replacing them with positive ones. So if you're ready to start harnessing your superpower of confidence, let's get started.

BELIEVING IS SEEING: HOW YOUR THOUGHTS SHAPE YOUR REALITY

Have you ever heard the saying, "you are your own worst enemy?" It's so common that I'm not sure anyone even knows who said it first. The unfortunate thing is that, when it comes to self-confidence, that saying can ring far too true. This is because our thoughts and beliefs have a huge impact on our level of confidence. I'm sure you know what thoughts are - the things we think about ourselves and the world around us. They can be positive or negative, and they can influence how we feel about ourselves and our abilities. Our beliefs, on the other hand, are the deeply held ideas and values that we have about ourselves and the world. They are often shaped by our experiences and can be difficult to change.

The problem is that negative thoughts and beliefs can hold us back from reaching our full potential. If we believe that we're not good enough, that we'll never succeed, or that we're not worthy of love and respect, then we're likely to feel anxious, insecure, and inadequate. And when we feel that way, we're less likely to take risks, speak up for ourselves, and pursue our goals and dreams.

After laying all of that concerning negativity on you, I'm happy to say that I do have some good news. You have the power and ability to change your thoughts and beliefs. You can learn to identify the negative thoughts and beliefs that are holding you back and replace them with more positive and empowering ones. By picking up this book, you are already well on your way to learning how to do this and much, much more.

MIND OVER MATTER: HOW TO IDENTIFY AND OVERCOME NEGATIVE SELF-TALK

Identifying and confronting negative thoughts is an essential step in building self-confidence and overcoming self-doubt. It's important to become aware of negative thoughts and beliefs, so you can challenge and replace them with more positive and accurate ones. One effective way to identify negative thoughts is through thought awareness exercises. These exercises involve paying close attention to your thoughts and feelings and writing them down as they come, without judging or analyzing them. This can help you become more aware of negative thoughts that may be holding you back.

For example, you might set aside 10-15 minutes of quiet time where you won't be interrupted. Grab a pen and a piece of paper or a journal, and sit comfortably. Take a few deep breaths to relax, and begin to notice the thoughts that come into your mind. Write them down as they come, without judging or analyzing them. Once you have a few thoughts written down, review them and look for any patterns or recurring themes. Be kind and patient with yourself in these moments, especially if you notice that your thoughts may tend toward the negative.

Another way to identify negative thoughts is to pay attention to your emotions. If you notice that you're feeling anxious, stressed, or overwhelmed, take a moment to consider what thoughts might be contributing to those feelings. Are you thinking negative or self-critical thoughts? Are you assuming the worst-case scenario? By becoming more aware of the thoughts that contribute to negative emotions, you can start to challenge and replace them with more positive and accurate ones.

Confronting negative thoughts involves questioning and challenging them. Once you've identified a negative thought, ask yourself if it's accurate and helpful. What evidence do you have to support this thought? What evidence do you have that contradicts it? Is there another way to interpret the situation? By questioning and challenging negative thoughts, you can start to see them in a more realistic and positive light. You're basically training your brain to react in a more healthy and positive manner, and it will get easier the more you do it.

Becoming aware of and confronting negative thoughts is an important step in building self-confidence and overcoming self-doubt. Thought awareness exercises and questioning negative thoughts can be powerful tools in this process. In the next section, we'll explore some common thought patterns that lead to negative beliefs, and how to recognize and confront them.

SHADES OF GRAY: OVERCOMING ALL-OR-NOTHING THINKING

As we've discussed, negative thoughts and beliefs can be incredibly powerful and can hold us back from reaching our full potential. One way to identify and confront negative thoughts is to recognize common thought patterns that can lead to negative beliefs.

One common thought pattern is all-or-nothing thinking. This is when we see things as black or white, with no shades of gray in between. For example, if we don't get an A on a test, we might think "I'm a failure" instead of acknowledging that we did our best and can learn from our mistakes. All-or-nothing thinking can lead to extreme and unrealistic expectations, which can set us up for disappointment and failure.

Another common thought pattern is jumping to conclusions, where we assume the worst without any evidence to support it. If someone doesn't respond to our text message right away, we might assume that they're mad at us or don't like us (or maybe that's just me and my anxiety talking). Jumping to conclusions can lead to unnecessary anxiety and stress, and can strain relationships. Trust me, I've been there and done that, and I'd love to save you the trouble.

Overgeneralization is another common thought pattern that can lead to negative beliefs. This is when we make sweeping negative statements based on a single event or piece of evidence. For example, if we fail one math test, we might think "I'm terrible at math" instead of recognizing that we can learn from our mistakes and improve. Writing this book has made me acutely aware of just how horrible my thoughts toward myself were as a teenager. I really hope you can benefit from my struggles and lessons learned, though. I could see a world in which that made it all worthwhile.

Recognizing these common thought patterns can help us become more aware of negative thoughts and beliefs that may be holding us back. By challenging and replacing these negative thoughts with more positive and accurate ones, we can break free from the cycle of self-doubt and reach our full potential.

MIND GAMES: REPLACING NEGATIVE THOUGHTS WITH POSITIVE ONES

Negative thoughts, full potential, blah, blah, blah. I know I sound like a broken record, but that is because it is so important to understand just how damaging negative thoughts and self-talk can be. They can make us feel anxious, self-conscious, and insecure, and can prevent us from pursuing our dreams and goals. They can convince us that we do not deserve good things and lead to self-sabotage. They're a hard thing to let go of, despite all of this. However, with practice and effort, we can learn to replace negative thoughts with positive ones and develop a more confident mindset.

One effective technique for replacing negative thoughts with positive ones is cognitive reframing. Cognitive reframing involves questioning and challenging negative thoughts and replacing them with more positive and accurate ones. For example, instead of thinking "I'm not good enough," we can reframe that thought to "I'm doing my best, and I can learn from my mistakes." By questioning and challenging negative thoughts, we can break free from all-or-nothing thinking, jumping to conclusions, and overgeneralization, replacing them with positive thought patterns that will contribute to our long-term happiness and wellness.

Another powerful technique for replacing negative thoughts with positive ones is positive self-talk. Positive self-talk is the process of intentionally talking to ourselves in a positive and encouraging way, just like we would talk to a friend who needs support. This technique can help us challenge negative beliefs, build self-confidence, and develop a more positive outlook on life. Examples of positive self-talk include "I am capable and competent," "I am worthy of love and respect," and "I can handle any challenge that comes my way."

Visualization is another valuable technique for replacing negative thoughts with positive ones that involves imagining ourselves succeeding in a given situation. This can help us overcome fear and anxiety, build self-confidence, and develop a more positive and optimistic mindset. For example, if we're nervous about a public speaking engagement, we can visualize ourselves delivering the speech with confidence and poise.

To effectively replace negative thoughts with positive ones, it's important to identify the negative thoughts and beliefs that are holding us back. This can be done through thought awareness exercises, such as journaling or mindfulness meditation. By becoming more aware of our thoughts and feelings, we can identify negative patterns and challenge them with positive reframes and self-talk.

It's also important to practice these techniques consistently, both in moments of stress and in our everyday lives. By incorporating positive self-talk, visualization, and cognitive reframing into our daily routine, we can build a more positive and confident mindset, which in turn will make our lives happier and healthier.

AFFIRM YOUR WAY TO CONFIDENCE: A GUIDE TO POSITIVE SELF-TALK

Positive affirmations are simple yet powerful statements that can help to build self-confidence and cultivate a positive mindset. These statements are repeated regularly to shift beliefs and attitudes about oneself and their abilities. It can feel kind of silly at first to tell yourself these things, but the human brain is a funny thing. This is the part where you metaphorically "fake it 'til you make it." Here are some examples of effective affirmations:

- "I am becoming more confident each day, and I trust in my abilities to handle whatever challenges come my way."

- "I am worthy of love and respect."

- "I am capable of achieving my goals and living my dreams."

- "I am filled with inner strength and resilience."

- "I am surrounded by abundance and prosperity."

It's important to make affirmations specific and realistic, acknowledging where you are currently while still affirming your potential to grow and improve. Using present tense language creates a sense of immediacy and urgency, making the affirmation feel like it is already true in the present moment. Consistency and regularity are also key factors in the effectiveness of affirmations. Incorporating them into your daily routine can be done by repeating them silently to yourself in the morning, writing them in a journal, or displaying them somewhere visible like a sticky note on your mirror.

Affirmations can be particularly helpful for addressing specific areas of self-doubt or insecurity. For example, if you struggle with social anxiety, you might use affirmations like "I am calm and relaxed in social situations" or "I am confident in my ability to connect with others." Visualization can be a powerful technique for building self-confidence when used in conjunction with affirmations. By visualizing yourself succeeding in a given situation while repeating positive affirmations, you can create a strong sense of self-belief and prepare yourself for success. In the words of the immortal Little Engine That Could, "I think I can!"

And with that, you've survived the first chapter. Congrats! In the next chapter, we'll be shifting our focus to self acceptance by exploring varying ways to cultivate self-love and compassion, including practicing gratitude for the things you have, accepting and appreciating your imperfections, and focusing on self-care. By learning to love and accept ourselves for who we are, we can build a foundation of confidence and resilience that will serve us well throughout our lives.

MAIN POINTS

- It is important to challenge negative thoughts and beliefs and replace them with positive ones.

- Thought awareness exercises, combined with paying close attention to your emotions, can help you identify negative thought patterns.

- Common negative thought patterns include all-or-nothing thinking, jumping to conclusions, and overgeneralization.

- Effective techniques for replacing negative thoughts with positive ones include cognitive reframing, positive self-talk, and visualization.

- Positive affirmations are an important tool to combat negative thoughts, self-doubt, and insecurity.

HERE`S A GIFT FOR YOU

Thank you so much for purchasing this book!
Since your parents may have purchased this amazing
guidebook for you, go ahead and give them this gift.
And surely we didn't forget to give you a little
something extra either! We hope you enjoy filling in
our self-esteem workbook and discover more about
yourself.

AND BEST OF ALL.. WE`RE GIVING YOU A THE FREE AUDIOBOOK VERSION!

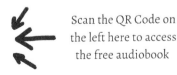

Scan the QR Code on
the left here to access
the free audiobook

2.

PERFECTLY IMPERFECT:

EMBRACING YOURSELF, FLAWS AND ALL

"Love yourself first and everything else falls into line. You really have to love yourself to get anything done in this world."
-Lucille Ball

And just like that, we're back with another chapter on building confidence and self-esteem. You're still here, so you must have found something that kept you going. Maybe it was an idea or a sudden realization or my impeccable writing skills. The world may never know. The important thing is that you're still here, which means you're ready to continue on in this process of growth and discovery. In the last chapter, we talked about the power of positive affirmations and how they can help you replace negative thoughts with positive ones. Now, we're going to focus on something equally important: learning to love yourself just the way you are.

It's easy to fall into the trap of comparing ourselves to others, whether it's our friends, celebrities, or people we see on social media. We might think, "If only I had her body" or "If only I were as talented as him." Really, the truth is that comparing ourselves to others only leads to feelings of inadequacy and self-doubt. It's important to remember that everyone has their own unique strengths and weaknesses, and that's what makes us who we are. Learning to love yourself as you are doesn't mean that you should stop striving for self-improvement or personal growth. It means accepting yourself for who you are in this moment, flaws and all. When you love and accept yourself, you're more likely to take care of yourself, set healthy boundaries, and pursue your dreams with confidence and purpose.

As you read on, you will encounter some nifty tips and strategies for cultivating self-love and acceptance. We'll also talk about the importance of self-care and setting boundaries, the power of gratitude and self-compassion, and how to overcome negative self-talk. By the end of this chapter, you'll have a better understanding of what it means to love yourself as you are, and how to apply that love and acceptance to your daily life.

IDENTITY CRISIS: NAVIGATING THE CHALLENGES OF TEENAGE SELF-DISCOVERY

Understanding your sense of self and identity is a crucial step towards self-love and self-acceptance. Your sense of self is made up of various aspects that make you unique and individual. These aspects include your personality traits, interests, values, beliefs, culture, and experiences. Understanding and accepting these aspects can help you develop a more positive relationship with yourself and build self-confidence.

Personality traits are the characteristics that define who you are. They can include your strengths and weaknesses, your preferences, and your unique quirks. Embracing your personality traits can help you appreciate your individuality and celebrate the things that make you different.

As I am sure you know, interests are the things that you enjoy doing, whether it's a hobby, sport, or activity. You probably don't need the definition, but there it is (just in case). Pursuing your interests can bring you joy and fulfillment and help you develop a stronger sense of self.

Values are the principles and beliefs that guide your behavior and decision-making. They reflect what is important to you and what you stand for. Understanding and aligning your actions with your values can help you feel more confident and fulfilled in your choices.

Beliefs refer to your ideas and opinions about the world and yourself. These beliefs can be positive or negative and can greatly impact your sense of self. Challenging negative beliefs and replacing them with positive ones can help you build self-confidence and a more positive self-image.

Culture refers to the customs, traditions, and beliefs of a particular group or society. Your cultural background can shape your sense of self and impact how you perceive yourself and the world around you.

Experiences are the events and circumstances that you have encountered throughout your life. These experiences shape your perspective and contribute to your unique sense of self. Embracing and learning from experiences (be they positive or negative) will help you develop a stronger sense of resilience and self-awareness, which are very important in building and maintaining self-confidence.

In order to fully develop your sense of self and continue building self-confidence, you have to understand (and accept) all of the tiny moving parts that comprise who you are. It's important to remember that your sense of self is not fixed and can (and should) evolve and change over time. By embracing who you are and exploring new aspects of yourself, you can cultivate a positive relationship with yourself and continue to grow and develop. This is what you should strive for, as stagnation is not good for anyone involved.

BREAKING FREE: REMOVING LABELS THAT LIMIT US

Labels can be both positive and negative. They can give us a sense of identity, or they can strip us of our sense of self and hold us back. "Smart" or "athletic" can feel positive, but it can also create pressure to live up to those expectations. "The pretty one" can seem like a compliment, but it usually also means that you aren't "the smart one" or "the funny one." Being labeled as "shy" or "awkward" can feel negative upfront, and can also create a self-fulfilling prophecy where we start to believe that we're not capable of socializing or making friends. It's important to recognize when labels are limiting us. This is when it is time to remove them from our self-concept. Now, this doesn't mean that we should deny parts of our identity or ignore our strengths and weaknesses. Rather, it means that we should focus on the qualities that we value and that make us unique, rather than on labels that others have placed on us.

One way to remove limiting labels is to reframe them in a positive way. For example, instead of thinking of yourself as "shy" or "awkward," you can reframe that label to "thoughtful" or "observant." By reframing the label in a positive way, you can start to see yourself in a more positive light and focus on your strengths. Another way to remove limiting labels is to focus on aspects of your identity that are important to you. These might include your values, interests, or hobbies. By focusing on the things that you care about, you can start to see yourself as a complex and multifaceted individual, rather than someone who is defined by a single label.

Here are some aspects of identity to consider when trying to remove limiting labels:

- Values: What do you believe in? What's important to you?

- Interests: What activities or hobbies do you enjoy? What do you like to learn about?

- Personality: What are your unique personality traits? How do they positively or negatively influence your interactions with others?

- Relationships: Who are the important people in your life? How do they influence your sense of self?

- Goals: What do you want to achieve in your life? What motivates you?

By focusing on these aspects of identity, you can start to see yourself as a whole person, rather than being defined by a single label. This can help you remove limiting beliefs and live a more fulfilling life.

THE COMPARISON GAME: HOW TO STOP PLAYING AND START LOVING YOURSELF

Comparing ourselves to others is a natural human tendency. From a young age, we learn to compare ourselves to others and measure our success and worth against theirs. While some comparison can be healthy and motivating, constantly comparing ourselves to others can have a negative impact on our self-esteem and confidence.

One reason why we compare ourselves to others is because we live in a society that values achievement and success. We're taught that being the best and achieving more than others is the key to happiness and fulfillment. This can lead us to constantly compare ourselves to others, feeling inadequate if we don't measure up to their achievements. Another reason why we compare ourselves to others is because of social media. With the rise of social media platforms, it's easier than ever to compare ourselves to others. We constantly see carefully curated and filtered posts of people's lives, highlighting only the best parts. This can make us feel like we're not doing enough, not successful enough, or not living our lives to the fullest.

The problem with constant comparison is that it can lead to equally constant negative self-talk and self-doubt. When we endlessly compare ourselves to others, we focus on our own perceived flaws and shortcomings, rather than our strengths and accomplishments. This can create a vicious cycle of self-doubt and insecurity, preventing us from reaching our full potential. To overcome the negative impact of the comparison trap, it's important to focus on your own journey and progress, rather than comparing yourself to others. Here are some tips for overcoming the comparison trap:

- **Recognize the negative impact of constant comparison:** The first step in overcoming the comparison trap is to recognize the negative impact it has on our self-esteem and confidence. By staying aware of how comparison affects us, we can start to take steps to overcome it.

- **Practice gratitude:** Gratitude can be a powerful tool for negating the effects of comparison. By focusing on what we have and what we've accomplished, we can shift our focus from what we lack to what we've achieved. Practicing gratitude regularly can help us develop a more positive and optimistic outlook on life. It is something that also gets easier with practice, so don't panic if it seems difficult at first.

- **Celebrate your own successes:** Instead of comparing ourselves to others, it's important to focus on our own journey and progress. Take time to celebrate your own successes, no matter how small they may seem.

Someone out there would think that your small accomplishment is a huge deal. Recognize and appreciate your own accomplishments, rather than measuring them against others'.

- **Limit social media use:** Social media can be a major contributor to the comparison trap. Limiting your social media use, or taking a break from it altogether, can help you focus on your own journey and progress, rather than constantly comparing yourself to others.

- **Surround yourself with positive influences:** Surrounding yourself with positive influences, such as supportive friends and family, can help you stay focused on your own journey and progress. Seek out people who encourage and support you, rather than those who constantly compare and compete with you.

By focusing on our own journey and progress, practicing gratitude, celebrating our own successes, limiting social media use, and surrounding ourselves with positive influences, we can overcome the negative impact of constant comparison and build a more positive and confident sense of self. Which, I will admit, is all way easier said than done.

BEYOND WHAT MEETS THE EYE: THE IMPACT OF BODY IMAGE ON CONFIDENCE AND SELF-ESTEEM

Body image is a term that describes how you feel about your physical appearance, including your size, shape, and features. It encompasses your thoughts, feelings, and beliefs about your body, as well as your perception of how others view your body.For many teenagers, body image can be a massive source of stress and insecurity, especially with the prevalence of social media and seemingly constant exposure to idealized and often unrealistic beauty standards. These standards can be perpetuated by media and advertising, peer pressure, and even family and cultural expectations.

Negative body image can be incredibly detrimental to self-esteem and confidence, often leading to feelings of inadequacy, self-doubt, and anxiety. This can manifest in various ways, including (but not limited to) engaging in unhealthy dieting behaviors, excessively exercising, or even developing body dysmorphic disorder (BDD), a mental health condition characterized by an obsessive preoccupation with perceived flaws or defects in one's appearance. When you don't like what you see in the mirror, it can be impossible to be happy in other aspects of your life.

One of the biggest challenges with body image is that it's often influenced by factors that are outside of our control. For example, we can't change our height, bone structure, or genetics (as much as we may wish we could). However, it's important to recognize that we can still work towards a positive body image and learn to appreciate and love our bodies for what they are.

Improving body image involves developing a positive relationship with our bodies, and this can involve a combination of strategies. This can mean challenging negative thoughts and beliefs about our bodies, practicing self-compassion and self-care, and engaging in activities that promote body positivity and acceptance.

It's important to remember that improving body image can be a process, and it's not always easy. It may take time, effort, and support from others, but it's always worth it. A positive body image can lead to greater self-confidence, improved mental health, and a happier, more fulfilling life. Who wouldn't want that?

DISTORTED REFLECTION: UNDERSTANDING BODY DYSMORPHIA

Negative body image can have severe consequences for mental and physical health. In some cases, it can lead to body dysmorphia or eating disorders, which can have long-lasting effects on a person's well-being.

Body dysmorphia is a mental health disorder characterized by a fixation on perceived flaws in one's appearance, regardless of how they are viewed by anyone else. This can lead to extreme anxiety and low self-esteem, which can impact a person's daily life, relationships, and overall happiness.

Eating disorders, such as anorexia nervosa, bulimia nervosa, and binge eating disorder, are serious conditions that involve unhealthy eating habits and behaviors. They can be triggered by a variety of factors, including negative body image, low self-esteem, and societal pressure to be thin. Eating disorders can lead to a range of physical and mental health problems, including malnutrition, organ damage, and depression. It is incredibly important for you to seek adult help if you or someone you know is suffering from any of these illnesses.

Negative body image can also lead to a range of behaviors that put a person's health at risk, such as over-exercising, fad dieting, and even substance abuse. Science has proven time and time again that the most important part of any diet is simply proper portioning. Our bodies are not designed to handle extreme dieting. These behaviors can have both short-term and long-term consequences, including physical injury, weakened immune system, and even death.

Everyone is unique and has a different body shape and size. There is no one "ideal" body type, despite what societal standards may suggest. Focusing on health, rather than appearance, can lead to a happier and more fulfilling life.

BEAUTY IN DIVERSITY: CELEBRATING YOUR UNIQUE BODY AND IDENTITY

Now that we've explored some of the negative effects that poor body image can have on our mental and physical well-being, let's shift our focus to how we can improve our body image and develop a more positive relationship with our bodies. With practice and effort, it's possible to learn to appreciate and love our bodies for what they are instead of hating them for what they aren't.

One important step in improving body image is to stop worrying so much about how we look and to think more about all the cool stuff our body does. Rather than obsessing over how we look, we can focus on the ways in which our bodies allow us to move, experience the world, and connect with others. This shift in perspective can help us to appreciate our bodies for all that they do for us, rather than fixating on their flaws. I know this kind of thinking really helped me a few years back.

Your body does everything for you, and I am always marveling over this fact now. I had to have knee surgery while I was in college (I apparently tore my meniscus years prior and just never knew, which is kind of typical of my luck), and I remember being so frustrated at the pain and difficulty associated with the recovery process. I was angry with my body for the things it couldn't do and the things it was putting me through. I had to learn to drive with both feet because I couldn't even pivot my right foot from gas to brake pedal. It was infuriating and embarrassing. I don't remember who, or I'd thank them a thousand times over, but somebody put everything into perspective for me one day. They told me that my body was doing everything it could for me, and I should be grateful for the fact that I can do things like see, hear, breathe, and walk (even though it hurt like hell to do so). They were right. It may have been struggling to do one thing, but my body was doing so many incredible things for me, and I didn't even care enough to see it. Flipping that perspective on its head was the best thing I could've done for my relationship with my own body.

Another important step in improving body image is to surround ourselves with positive messages and role models. This can include following social media accounts that promote body positivity and diversity, reading books and articles that celebrate different body types, and seeking out friends and mentors who encourage us to embrace our bodies and feel confident in our own skin.

It's also important to practice self-care and self-compassion. This includes prioritizing activities that make us feel good, such as exercise, spending time in nature, or practicing meditation. It also means treating ourselves with kindness and compassion, rather than harshly criticizing ourselves for perceived flaws or imperfections.

I know I said it once already, but seeking professional help can be an important step for those who struggle with body dysmorphia, eating disorders, or other serious body image issues. Professional therapists, nutritionists, and other healthcare professionals can provide guidance and support for those who need it. They are trained to do so in ways that are compassionate, safe, and judgment free.

As we wrap up this chapter, it's important to remember that developing a positive relationship with your body takes time and effort. It's not always easy to change deeply ingrained beliefs and thought patterns, but with practice and patience, it is possible to improve your body image and build a more positive sense of self. Just as it's important to have a healthy relationship with ourselves and our bodies, it's also important to have healthy relationships with others. In the next chapter, we'll explore the importance of setting boundaries in our relationships and how it can contribute to our overall well-being.

MAIN POINTS

- Comparison can be detrimental to your self-esteem and mental health.

- You must develop an understanding of yourself and your identity in order to fully love and accept who you are.

- Labels can be positive or negative, so be wary of letting them define you too heavily.

- Body image can drastically influence your self-confidence.

- Body dysmorphia is a mental health disorder that should be taken very seriously and treated by the proper medical professionals.

- The unique nature of personal identity is what makes you so amazing - you will always be the best version of you out there.

3.

FENCES MAKE GREAT NEIGHBORS:

HOW BOUNDARIES CAN BOOST YOUR SELF-ESTEEM

"Boundaries are a part of self-care. They are healthy, normal, and necessary." - Doreen Virtue

In this chapter, I want to talk to you about something that I wish I had learned about much sooner than I did: setting healthy boundaries. I know it might not seem like a big deal right now, but trust me, it's something you'll be grateful for in the long run. As you're growing up, you're going to encounter all sorts of people and situations that may make you uncomfortable or uncertain. That's where boundaries come in. By setting boundaries, you are communicating to others that you value yourself and are in control of your life and what is in it.

So, why are boundaries especially important for teenagers? Well, for starters, this is a time in your life when you're figuring out who you are and what you stand for, which is a pretty big deal. Setting boundaries helps you establish your identity and teaches others how to treat you. It also helps you to develop self-respect and self-worth, so the earlier you start, the better off you'll be. Another reason why boundaries are important is that they can work to protect you from harm by making it clear that you won't tolerate mistreatment or abuse from anyone. There are a lot of people in the world who will try to take advantage of you if you let them. I'm definitely not saying everyone will, but it's better to set boundaries and not need them than need them and not have them. Boundaries also help you to maintain healthy relationships. When you're clear about what you will and won't accept from others, it's easier to build trust and respect. Your friends and family will appreciate your honesty and will know that you value yourself enough to stand up for yourself.

Another aspect of setting boundaries is that it helps you prioritize your time and energy. As a teenager, you likely have a lot of obligations and activities that demand your attention, such as schoolwork, extracurricular activities, family responsibilities, and social events. When you set boundaries, you give yourself permission to say "no" to things that don't align with your values or goals, or that would simply drain your energy or stress you out. By doing this, you free up time and mental space for the things that truly matter to you. I even have a super nifty example just for this purpose! Let's say you've been invited to a party on a school night, but you know you have a big test the next day.

Setting a boundary in this situation might mean saying "no" to the party, even if your friends are going. It can be hard to turn down fun opportunities, but by prioritizing your education and setting boundaries around your study time, you're setting yourself up for success in the long run.

TAKING INVENTORY: ASSESSING YOUR EMOTIONAL AND PHYSICAL BOUNDARIES

Now that we've talked about why boundaries are important, let's move on to how to identify your own boundaries. Wondering how the heck to navigate this process? Don't worry, you won't have to figure it out alone. The first thing you need to do is to take a look at your own values and beliefs. What's important to you? What do you stand for? What are your deal-breakers? Once you have a clear understanding of your own values, you can start to set boundaries that align with them. For example, you might value honesty, kindness, and respect, and feel uncomfortable when people lie to you, treat you poorly, or invade your personal space. Another way to identify your boundaries is to pay attention to your emotions. If someone is making you feel uncomfortable, anxious, or stressed out, it might be a sign that they're crossing a boundary. This is the time to trust your gut. If it helps, you may want to make a list as you work through these thoughts. I always felt like writing something down helped me think it through.

Once you've identified your values and needs, you can start thinking about how to communicate your boundaries to others. It's important to do this clearly and assertively. This can be a tough part of the process because you don't want to come across as aggressive or confrontational, but you also don't want to let people walk all over you. Don't be afraid to speak up for yourself and let others know what you will and won't accept. It might feel uncomfortable at first, but it's an important skill to develop, and there are ways to navigate the situation much easier. One strategy is to use "I" statements, such as "I feel uncomfortable when you do/say X" or "I need Y in order to feel safe/happy/etc." Think about how you would feel hearing that instead of "You always make me feel X" or "You need to do Y for me." "I" statements place the focus on your own feelings and needs, rather than making it seem like the other person is doing something wrong. This is a lesson that has helped greatly in my own communication with others, and I wish I had learned it sooner.

It's also important to remember that setting boundaries is an ongoing process. You might need to adjust your boundaries depending on the situation or the person you're dealing with. For example, you might be comfortable with a physical touch from close friends or family members, but not from acquaintances or strangers. Or, you might be okay with joking around with your friends, but not with people who make mean or offensive comments. Even recently, I realized that I am okay with certain jokes when my boyfriend makes them, but not when other people do. We are very close and it does not feel hurtful when he teases me because I know it is not coming from a hurtful place. I have learned so much about myself through the process of analyzing (and re-analyzing) how situations make me feel and what my boundaries are in all of my relationships, including the one I have with myself.

In addition to protecting your time and energy, setting boundaries can also boost your self-esteem and confidence. When you set boundaries and enforce them, you show yourself and others that you value yourself and your needs. This can be especially important if you've struggled with low self-esteem or confidence in the past. I used to be so annoyed when my parents would tell me that I needed to respect myself in order to be respected by others. I thought it was ridiculous to imply that you don't deserve respect if you struggle with self-worth. I realized as an adult that I had completely misunderstood what they were meaning to say. The reason that self-confidence is tied to the way you are treated is simply to do with boundaries. If you love and respect yourself, you will have the courage and confidence to set healthy boundaries to ensure you are treated in the way that you deserve. Conversely, if you don't set boundaries or allow others to cross them, it can lead to feelings of resentment, anger, and low self-esteem. You might start to feel like you don't matter or that your needs aren't important.

I know we've already kind of touched on some examples of boundaries and how to discover your own, but I also want to emphasize that boundaries do not have to be only physical and emotional. Here I'd like to provide you with some examples of healthy boundaries that you can set, along with what you can do to communicate these to your friends and loved ones. Keep in mind, this is not a complete list! If you have a boundary that isn't listed here, congrats! You did the work to figure it out, and that's awesome.

Personal Space: This boundary is about physical touch and personal space. It's important to communicate with others about what we feel comfortable with in terms of physical touch, such as hugs or high-fives. For example, you might tell someone that you don't like to be hugged by strangers or that you only like to give high-fives to your friends. I always make sure my kids know that they don't have to hug anyone that they don't want to, no matter who it is - including me and my family. If you are in a situation where someone tries to touch you and you are uncomfortable, you can simply say "I would prefer not to be touched. Thank you!" If this doesn't work, don't hesitate to find a trusted adult and explain that your physical boundaries are not being respected.

Time Management: This boundary focuses on your time and how you spend it. It's important to prioritize your own needs and make time for the things that are important to you. If you give too much of yourself to other plans, you will wear yourself out. For example, if you feel overwhelmed with schoolwork and extracurricular activities, you might say no to going out with friends on a weeknight in order to focus on your homework. Especially while in college, I turned down plenty of offers to go places because I either needed to work on homework or just needed time to relax and decompress. If you are invited to do something but are unable to go (or just don't want to), you may try saying something like "This doesn't fit into my schedule right now, but I appreciate you inviting me. Maybe we can make plans when I have more free time!"

Social Media and Technology Use: This boundary is about how we use technology and social media. It's important to use these tools in a way that feels healthy and balanced for us. For example, you might choose to turn off notifications on your phone so that you can focus on your homework without getting distracted by texts and social media updates. If you are talking to someone and want to communicate this, you could tell them "I am going to focus on homework right now. I will talk to you later!" This is something I sucked at in my early college years, but my grades saw the benefit once I learned to respect and manage my time better.

Communication: This boundary is about how we communicate with others. It's important to communicate our thoughts and feelings honestly and respectfully. For example, you might tell a friend that you don't feel comfortable talking about a certain topic or that you need some alone time to recharge. My friends and family are very understanding when I say that I need some time to myself or that I don't want to talk about something. It makes talking to them much less stressful because I know that I am being respected.

Personal Beliefs: This boundary is about our own beliefs and values. It's important to respect ourselves and others by setting boundaries around conversations or actions that go against our beliefs. For example, we might choose to avoid conversations about politics or religion with someone who has different views than us. Especially with how hectic the world has been, I've found myself avoiding certain topics, like politics or the pandemic, when I feel like it will lead to conflict. I've had a lot of success with a simple "I don't want to talk about X, please, it is a stressful topic that I would rather avoid" followed by a new topic to redirect the conversation.

Emotional Boundaries: This boundary is about how we allow others to treat us emotionally. It's important to be aware of how we feel and to communicate our needs in order to maintain healthy relationships. For example, we might tell someone that we don't appreciate being talked down to or that we need space when we're feeling upset. Especially in arguments or serious conversations, I tend to get emotionally overwhelmed. One thing that has been very helpful is learning to say "Hey, I need to remove myself from this situation for a moment in order to calm down. I would like to resume this conversation after a short break." This ensures that the other person does not feel ignored while also ensuring that my emotional needs are met.

Remember, these are only a few examples! If you need help communicating a boundary, it can help to ask a parent or a trusted friend how you could best get your needs across. I know it's helped me!

STANDING YOUR GROUND: ENFORCING BOUNDARIES WHEN OTHERS DON'T RESPECT THEM

It is important to remember that your boundaries can (and will) be different from the ones other people set for themselves. You are setting boundaries for yourself, not for anyone else. If someone has a problem with your boundaries, or does not respect them, it is time to reconsider whether that person respects and values you and your relationship enough to stay in your life. When I was 16 years old, I had a close friend - we'll call her Mary. I enjoyed spending time with Mary. We would hang out after school and on weekends, and generally I thought we had a lot of fun together. At first. As our friendship continued, I started to notice some problematic behaviors. Mary had a habit of making insensitive and hurtful comments about my appearance and my personality. She would often make fun of my weight, my clothing choices, and my hobbies. At first, I tried to ignore it or brush it off as harmless teasing, but as time went on, it started to wear on me. I realized that her comments were not only hurtful, but also disrespectful of my boundaries. I had never given her permission to make personal comments about me in this way, and it was starting to impact my self-esteem. I developed body image issues and was always dissatisfied with the way I looked. Suddenly I was self-conscious of sharing the things I enjoyed with others. Eventually, I couldn't handle how this was making me feel and I decided to confront her about the way she had been treating me.

Despite my attempts to address the issue with her, she continued to make these comments. I eventually realized that if I wanted to protect my mental and emotional well-being, I needed to set a clear boundary with her. So, I told her that I was no longer willing to tolerate her hurtful comments and that I needed her to stop. Unfortunately, my friend didn't take my boundary seriously and continued to make hurtful comments.

It was a difficult decision, but I eventually decided to end the friendship because I knew that it wasn't healthy for me to be around someone who didn't respect my boundaries. Looking back on that experience, I realize that it was a valuable lesson in the importance of setting and enforcing boundaries. It taught me that I have the right to protect my own mental and emotional well-being and that I should never compromise my own values and self-respect for the sake of a friendship.

BOUNDARIES AND BULLYING: WHY SAYING "NO" CAN BE THE MOST EMPOWERING RESPONSE

On a semi-related note, let's talk about how to use boundaries to deal with the bane of everyone's high school existence (besides that test you forgot to study for). Bullying is a real issue for people of every age, but it seems to be very common in high schools across the globe. Unfortunately, there are people in the world who will try to hurt or intimidate you. They thrive on making people feel small and helpless. This can be a scary and overwhelming experience, but setting boundaries can help you navigate it in a healthy way. It's important to remember that enforcing your boundaries does not mean you are inviting confrontation or being aggressive. Rather, it is about asserting your right to be treated with respect.

If you are being bullied, it's important to first try to remove yourself from the situation if possible. This can mean physically walking away or seeking the help of a trusted adult. If you feel comfortable doing so, you can also try calmly and assertively telling the bully that their behavior is not okay and that you will not tolerate it. Remember, bullies often thrive on power and control. By standing up for yourself and asserting your boundaries, you are taking away their power and sending a message that you will not be intimidated. It is also important to recognize when a situation may be too dangerous or overwhelming to handle on your own. If you ever feel that you are in danger, it's important to seek the help of a trusted adult or authority figure. There is no shame in asking for help when you need it - the most important thing in these situations is your safety.

Sometimes, setting boundaries with your bully doesn't stop them. Being bullied like this is a very difficult experience and can leave you struggling with your self-worth. I would like to take a moment here to explain some ways to move forward from these harmful encounters and regain your confidence. Below are some tips that might help:

Talk to someone: It's important to share your experience with someone you trust. This could be a friend, a family member, a teacher, or a school counselor. Talking about what happened can help you process your feelings and get support.

Don't blame yourself: Remember that being bullied is not your fault. Bullies often pick on others to feel better about themselves or because they're dealing with their own issues. It's important to recognize that the problem is with the bully and not with you.

Focus on your strengths: Instead of dwelling on your weaknesses or the negative things that the bully said, focus on your strengths and the things that make you unique. Remember that you have value and worth, regardless of what anyone else says or thinks.

Practice self-care: Take care of yourself by getting enough sleep, eating well, and engaging in activities that you enjoy. Exercise can also be a great way to boost your mood and confidence.

Surround yourself with positive people: Try to spend time with people who support and encourage you. Positive relationships can help you feel more confident and resilient.

Remember, healing takes time and everyone's journey is different. But by taking these steps, you can move forward from bullying and regain your self-confidence

All of this is to say, setting boundaries is an important skill to develop. It allows you to assert your needs and values, build healthy relationships, and protect yourself from unwanted or harmful situations. By identifying your own boundaries, recognizing their impact on your self-confidence, and learning how to use them in challenging situations, you can become more empowered and confident in all areas of your life. Nobody should ever make you feel hurt, unsafe, or invalidated. You deserve to be treated with respect, and setting boundaries is an important way to ensure that you are. Take this difficult step now, and enjoy the rest of your life knowing that you'll reap the benefits.

MAIN POINTS

- Boundaries are important because they help you establish your identity, teach others how to treat you, and help you develop self-respect and self-worth.

- In order to identify your own boundaries, you must evaluate your own values and beliefs and pay attention to your emotions.

- It is also important to communicate your boundaries to others in a healthy and effective manner.

- Boundaries can be used to protect yourself from bullies.

- Setting boundaries is an ongoing process, not a one-time thing.

4.

THE POWER OF PURPOSE:

DISCOVERING YOUR 'WHY'

"The two most important days in your life are the day you are born and the day you find out why." - Mark Twain

Have you ever felt like you're going through the motions of life without a clear sense of purpose or direction? Maybe you're doing well in school or your hobbies, but deep down, you feel unfulfilled or unmotivated? If you're mentally nodding at any of these, you're not alone. As a teenager, it's common to struggle with finding your place in the world and figuring out what you want to do with your life. But I want to let you in on a little secret: the key to doing all of this lies in uncovering your true purpose and passion. It all starts with discovering your "why" - that driving force that gives your life meaning and direction. In this chapter, we'll explore the importance of finding your "why" and I'll guide you through the process of uncovering your unique purpose and set you on the path to a fulfilling and meaningful life. So, let's dive in!It's all about discovering your why - that deep-seated motivation that drives you to do what you do. Think of it as your compass, guiding you toward a fulfilling and meaningful life. And I'm here to help you on this journey of self-discovery. So, let's sit down and have a heart-to-heart. Together, we'll explore your values, interests, and goals to uncover your "why" and set you on a path to success.

The process of finding your "why" can seem daunting at first, but it all starts with identifying your passions. Your passions are the things that make you feel alive, fulfilled, and excited about life. They're the things that you love to do and can get lost in for hours on end. Identifying your passions is crucial to discovering your "why" because it's the foundation of what motivates you to live a fulfilling and meaningful life. To identify your passions, start by asking yourself what you enjoy doing. Make a list of your favorite activities, subjects, hobbies, or whatever else I have missed that just sparks that flame inside you. Then, ask yourself why you love doing these things. Is it the challenge, the creativity, the sense of community? Understanding the "why" behind your passions is key to discovering your true purpose.

Next up, consider how your passions align with your values and goals. What matters most to you in life? What kind of impact do you want to have on the world? By aligning your passions with your values and goals, you'll find greater meaning and fulfillment in your life, and a fulfilled life is a happy life (or so I've been told). Here are some steps you can take to navigate this process:

- **Identify your values:** Make a list of your most important values. Maybe you value things like honesty, kindness, creativity, or perseverance. Think about why the values you identify matter to you and how you can incorporate them into your life.

- **Define your goals:** Take some time to think about what you want to achieve in life. Make a list of short-term and long-term goals that align with your values and passions. Remember to make your goals specific, measurable, achievable, relevant, and time-bound (SMART). The SMART-er your goals, the more likely you are to achieve them.

- **Find opportunities that align with your passions and goals:** This is the part where you find ways to pursue your passions and values. Identify different activities, clubs, groups, or courses that align with what you want to do. If you love cooking, see if there is a club for it at school or local cooking lessons. Or maybe you're a budding photographer - more and more schools offer classes on the arts, including digital and film photography. Seek out mentors or role models who can help guide you on your journey.

- **Take action:** Once you've identified your passions, values, and goals, it's time to take action, big time. Set specific actions or steps to work towards your goals. Break down the larger goals into smaller, manageable steps, and keep track of your progress. Celebrate the small wins along the way.

Setting passionate goals is a pivotal for discovering your "why." Goals give you direction and a sense of purpose, which in turn can boost your self-confidence and motivation. By setting goals that align with your passions, you'll find greater meaning in your life. One of the biggest benefits of setting goals is the clear sense of direction that they provide. Goals help you stay focused on what you want to achieve, and provide a roadmap for how to get there. This, in turn, can help build your self-confidence as you begin to make tangible progress. Another benefit of finding your purpose is the sense of fulfillment that accompanies it. When you have a clear purpose, you're able to see the bigger picture and understand how your actions fit into the larger plan. This can help give your life greater meaning and a sense of fulfillment.

FROM DOUBT TO PURPOSE: MY JOURNEY OF FINDING THE 'WHY' BEHIND MY PASSION

I know it might seem like I have a story for everything, but that's what makes me feel confident in offering insight to those who may need it. That being said, let me tell you about my own experience finding my "why." Ever since I was a young kid, I loved to write. I would spend hours scribbling down stories and ideas in notebooks, lost in my own imagination. But as I got older, I started to question whether writing was really a viable career path. Everyone around me seemed to be pursuing more practical professions, like medicine or law, and I began to worry that I was wasting my time with this hobby. I even started college on a pre-med track. Spoiler: that didn't last.

It wasn't until I participated in an open-mic night at my college that things started to change. I had poured my heart and soul into the poem I was going to read, and I was beyond terrified. Public speaking is bad enough without having to worry about whether your writing sucks too. To my surprise, everyone was raptly listening to the words I had woven together. When I finished, everyone was clapping and I was thrilled to be done with it. When I got back to my seat, I realized that people actually really liked what I had to say. That experience was a turning point for me. It showed me that writing wasn't just a frivolous pastime, but something that could be recognized and rewarded. I started to take my writing more seriously, seeking out classes and workshops to improve my skills.

Once I started writing about topics that truly mattered to me, I found my purpose as a writer. I realized that writing wasn't just something I enjoyed doing, but something that could make a real impact in the world. Now, as a young adult, I'm pursuing a career in writing, with the goal of using my words to make a difference. And while it's not always easy, I know that I'm following my true purpose, and that's a feeling that's hard to beat. Plus, it's super cool to tell people I am a published writer. The reactions are priceless.

TURNING DREAMS INTO REALITY: THE POWER OF SETTING AND ACHIEVING GOALS

So what do you do after finding your passion? You aren't always great at what you want to do right away and those who are can improve and refine their skills. This is where goal-setting comes into play. By setting meaningful and realistic goals for yourself, you can plan your journey to accomplishment and you'll be more motivated to achieve them and more likely to succeed in the long run. Of course, that isn't to say that this whole process is easy. If I did that, I'd be a total liar. It can take time and effort to figure out what truly drives you and what you want to achieve in life. But the journey is just as important as the destination. By taking small steps in the right direction, every day, you'll make progress and build momentum over time. And when you finally achieve your goals, the sense of satisfaction and fulfillment will make it all worth the wait.

As we established a moment ago, it's important to set goals for yourself that are both challenging and attainable. Here are some techniques for setting goals that are both achievable and meaningful:

- **Focus on short-term and long-term goals:** Short-term goals can help you build momentum and achieve quick wins, while long-term goals can give you a sense of direction and purpose over the long haul.

- **Align your goals with your passions and personal values:** This is crucial for setting goals that are truly meaningful to you. When your goals are aligned with your passions and values, you'll be more motivated to achieve them, and you'll feel a greater sense of fulfillment when you do.

- **Use the SMART goal setting framework:** SMART stands for Specific, Measurable, Achievable, Relevant, and Time-bound. Using this framework can help you set goals that are clear, focused, and realistic.

Despite sounding like goals with an above average IQ, the SMART goal setting framework is a widely used technique for setting realistic goals that you will stick to. Here's a breakdown of each component of the framework:

1. Specific: Your goal should be clear and specific, so that you know exactly what you're working towards.

2. Measurable: Your goal should be quantifiable, so that you can track your progress and determine whether you've achieved it.

3. Achievable: Your goal should be realistic and attainable. This keeps you from feeling discouraged or overwhelmed.

4. Relevant: Your goal should be relevant to your overall purpose and aligned with your passions and values. Otherwise, you may question why you are working toward it.

5. Time-bound: Time-bound: Your goal should have a specific deadline. A clear sense of urgency will limit procrastination or putting off progress for another time. Plus, you can track your progress over time, which feels really good to look back on.

By using the SMART goal setting framework and aligning your goals with your passions and personal values, you'll set goals that are both challenging and attainable, and that give you a sense of direction. Remember to focus on both short-term and long-term goals, be realistic and patient, and celebrate your progress along the way. With dedication, hard work, and a clear sense of purpose, you can achieve anything you set your mind to.

Tracking progress towards your goals is a crucial part of achieving them because who doesn't like a nice reminder of their progress? When you track your progress, you'll be able to see how far you've come, which can help you stay motivated and focused. Here are some techniques to track your progress and stay motivated:

- **Use a journal or planner:** Writing down your goals and tracking your progress in a journal or planner is a great way to stay organized and motivated. You can use your journal (or planner, whichever you prefer) to break down your goals into smaller, bite-sized tasks, and to track your progress towards each one. You don't even want to know how many smaller tasks writing this book consisted of.

- **Use a visual aid:** Creating a visual representation of your progress can be a powerful motivator. For example, you could create a totally color coordinated and overly decorated chart or graph that shows your progress over time, or you could use a habit tracker to monitor your daily progress. Without visual aids, it can feel like you aren't progressing at all sometimes.

- **Stay accountable:** Find someone who is willing to hold you accountable for your progress and pester you whenever you start slacking. This could be a friend, family member, or mentor who you trust to support and encourage you along the way.

Celebrating your achievements is also important for maintaining self-confidence and staying motivated. When you achieve a goal, take time to celebrate your success. Big, small, any size in between, it doesn't matter - a victory is a victory is a victory. Here are some ways you can celebrate your achievements:

- **Reflect on your progress:** It's good to take time to reflect on how far you've come and what you've accomplished. Recognize the effort and dedication it took to get there, especially from where you started, and give yourself credit for your hard work.

- **Treat yourself:** Do something special to celebrate your achievement. It doesn't have to be anything big. Taking yourself out for a nice meal or buying yourself a small gift are great ways to accomplish this.

- **Share your success:** Share your success with those who have supported you along the way. Let them know how much their support means to you, and how it helped you achieve your goal. They'll be thrilled to celebrate with you and will likely make you feel even more awesome for your accomplishments.

Like I said at the start of this section, tracking your progress towards your goals and celebrating your achievements are important steps in staying motivated and maintaining self-confidence. Journaling and visual aids, along with finding ways to celebrate your success, can help and encourage you to stay motivated and focused on achieving your goals. Remember to celebrate your progress, no matter how small, and to be patient and kind with yourself, even when you may not feel like you're winning.

MAIN POINTS

- Identify your passions: Make a list of your favorite activities, subjects, and hobbies, and ask yourself why you love doing these things.

- Align your passions with your values and goals: Identify your most important values and make a list of short-term and long-term goals that align with them. Find ways to pursue your passions and values through different activities, clubs, or courses.

- Set passionate goals: Set specific, measurable, achievable, relevant, and time-bound (SMART) goals that align with your passions. Break down larger goals into smaller, manageable steps, and track your progress.

- Take action: Once you've identified your passions, values, and goals, it's time to take action. Seek out mentors or role models who can help guide you, and celebrate the small wins along the way.

5.

FAILING FORWARD:

LEARNING AND GROWING FROM SETBACKS AND REJECTION

> *"A rejection is nothing more than a necessary step in the pursuit of success."* – Bo Bennett

Oftentimes, life can feel like a rollercoaster ride, full of ups and downs, twists and turns. One of the hardest things to deal with is failure and rejection, and trust me, I know it can feel like the end of the world. But here's the thing, it's not. Failure and rejection are a natural part of life, and they can actually be opportunities for growth and learning. In this chapter, we're going to talk about how to handle failure and rejection in a healthy way, so you can bounce back stronger and more resilient than ever before.

Failure and rejection can have a significant impact on a person's self-confidence. When we experience failure or rejection, we often internalize it as a personal flaw or inadequacy. We may feel like we're not good enough, not smart enough, not attractive enough, or not talented enough. Negative self-talk can eat away at you, leading to a decrease in self-esteem and self-worth. It can make you doubt yourself and your abilities, even things we logically know we aren't actually bad at. This can lead to a lack of motivation and a reluctance to try new things. As a teenager, it can be particularly challenging to deal with failure and rejection because you are still developing your sense of self and trying to figure out who you are. When you experience failure or rejection, it can make you question your identity and where you fit in the world. This can feel overwhelming and distressing, and it's important to take care of yourself during these difficult moments. However, it's also important to remember that failure and rejection are not personal attacks, and they do not define us as individuals. Instead, they are opportunities for growth and learning, and they can help us develop resilience and perseverance.

Dealing with setbacks is tough, and it can be especially difficult for teenagers. As a teen, you're likely facing a lot of pressure and stress from all directions. You're navigating school, relationships, and trying to figure out who you are and what you want to do with your life. When things don't go according to plan, it can feel like the world is falling apart. Here are some common challenges you might face when dealing with setbacks:

- **Feeling like a failure:** When you experience a setback, it's easy to feel like a failure. You might feel like you're not good enough or that you're never going to succeed. This can be a blow to your self-esteem and confidence, making it hard to bounce back.

- **Comparing yourself to others:** It's natural to compare yourself to others, but it can be particularly damaging when you're dealing with a setback. You might look at your peers and see how successful they are, which can make you feel even worse about yourself.

- **Fear of judgment:** Fear of judgment from others can also be a big challenge when dealing with setbacks. It is too easy to get caught up worrying about what your friends, family, or teachers will think if you fail. This fear can make it hard to take risks or try new things. Imagine a life where you never try anything new or exciting. How worthwhile could it be?

- **Giving up too easily:** When faced with a setback, it can be tempting to give up and throw in the towel. However, giving up too easily can lead to missed opportunities and regrets later on, and regret is a nasty burden to bear. It's important to learn how to persevere and keep trying, even when things get tough.

Remember, setbacks are a natural part of life. It's how you handle them that counts. By understanding the common challenges you might face and learning how to overcome them, you'll be better equipped to deal with setbacks and come out even stronger on the other side.

BUILDING RESILIENCE: HOW TO BOUNCE BACK FROM REJECTION

Experiencing failure or rejection can be tough, especially when you've put in a lot of effort and hoped for a positive outcome. However, it's important to remember that these experiences are a natural part of life and everyone goes through them. Following are some techniques for coping and learning from failure or rejection.

One of the best ways to cope with difficult emotions is through mindfulness. Mindfulness is a powerful tool for coping with difficult emotions. It involves being fully present in the moment, without judgment or distraction. When you practice mindfulness, you develop the ability to observe your thoughts and emotions without reacting to them. This can help you develop a sense of calm and acceptance, even in the face of failure or rejection. Exercises such as deep breathing, body scans, or meditation can help you practice mindfulness in your daily life.. One simple mindfulness exercise you can do anytime, anywhere, is to take a few deep breaths and focus on the sensations in your body. Notice the feeling of your breath moving in and out of your body, and the sensations in your chest and stomach. This can help you tune in to your body and quiet your mind, which can be especially helpful when you're feeling anxious or overwhelmed.

Self-compassion is imperative for coping with failure or rejection. By treating yourself with kindness, understanding, and compassion, just as you would a good friend who is going through a tough time, you are showing yourself that you matter. Acknowledging that everyone makes mistakes and experiences setbacks means that you are not alone in your struggles. To practice self-compassion, try speaking to yourself with the same kindness and understanding you would use with a friend. For example, you might say to yourself, "It's okay that you didn't get the outcome you wanted. Everyone makes mistakes, and you'll learn from this experience." You can also show yourself compassion by engaging in self-care activities, such as taking a relaxing bath, going for a walk in nature, or listening to your favorite music.

Self-reflection is the process of examining your own thoughts, feelings, and behaviors to gain a deeper understanding of yourself and your experiences, which can help you cope with failure and rejection. Recovering from setbacks can feel like an impossible feat, but it isn't - it's just a really unpleasant one.

When you experience failure or rejection, self-reflection can be a powerful tool for learning from the experience and making positive changes in the future. There are many different ways to engage in self-reflection, but here are some ideas to get you started:

1. Journaling: When reflecting on your experiences in a journal, try to be as honest and open as possible. Oh, and don't worry about grammar or spelling. Nobody else is meant to see what you write, unless you let them. You might find it helpful to write about what happened, how you felt about it, and what you learned from the experience.

2. Mindful reflection: Mindfulness exercises, such as meditation or deep breathing, can be used in moments of self-reflection to help you become more aware of your thoughts and emotions and gain a deeper understanding of yourself.

3. Talking to someone you trust: Sometimes it can be helpful to talk to someone you trust about your experiences, and they can help you reflect on them. It could be a friend, family member, or mental health professional, it really doesn't matter who you choose as long as they are willing to help. They can provide a different perspective on the situation, along with support and guidance.

When engaging in self-reflection, it's important to approach the process with a sense of curiosity and openness. Try to reserve any judgements and focus on learning from the experience. Here are some questions you might ask yourself:

- What happened? Describe the situation in detail.

- How did you feel about the situation? What emotions did you experience?

- What thoughts or beliefs do you have about the situation? Are these thoughts helpful or unhelpful?

- What did you learn from the experience? What could you do differently in the future?

Self-reflection provides you with a deeper understanding of yourself and your experiences. Even with all the reflection in the world, failure and rejection are a natural part of life that cannot be avoided forever. By learning from these experiences, you can become more resilient and better equipped to handle future challenges. The insights you gain through self-reflection can help you develop new skills, adjust your mindset, and make more informed decisions going forward. The insights you gain through self-reflection can help you develop new skills, adjust your mindset, and make more informed decisions in the future. Ultimately, self-reflection is a valuable tool for personal growth and can help you develop greater self-awareness and a deeper understanding of yourself and the world around you.

FROM SETBACKS TO COMEBACKS: NAVIGATING REJECTION AND FINDING YOUR WAY FORWARD

Setbacks are a natural part of life, and it's okay to feel down and disappointed when things don't go as planned. What's important is how you respond to those setbacks. It can be easy to dwell on the negative and give up, but there are strategies you can use to bounce back and move forward.

First, let's talk about setting new goals. When you experience a setback, it can be easy to feel lost or like you don't know what to do next. Totally valid feeling, too. I still get that way. However, setting new goals can help you regain focus and direction. Just make sure to take some time to reflect on what you really want. Ask yourself questions like: What are my values? What am I passionate about? What are my strengths and weaknesses? Use these answers to guide you in setting new goals that align with your interests and aspirations.

Next, let's look at discovering new opportunities that can help you turn a setback into something positive. For example, if you didn't get the job you wanted, consider volunteering or interning in a related field to gain more experience and make new connections. This can help you build new skills and expand your network, which can ultimately lead to more opportunities down the road. There is a reason that so many people believe that, when one door closes, another opens.

Perseverance is all about not giving up, even when things get tough. It's important to remember that it's okay to struggle or make mistakes. The key is to keep working towards your goals, even when it's difficult. In order to make them feel more manageable, consider breaking your goals down into smaller, more manageable steps, seeking support from others, and staying focused on the bigger picture. Resilience is closely related to perseverance, but it's more about being able to adapt to change and overcome setbacks than not giving up. When you experience a setback, it can be easy to get stuck in a negative mindset. That is why it is important to remind yourself that setbacks can also lead to new opportunities or perspectives. Being flexible and open to new experiences can help you bounce back more quickly and effectively when life gets in the way.

Having a growth mindset is unbelievably important for bouncing back from setbacks. A growth mindset means believing that your abilities and intelligence can be developed through hard work and dedication. This is in contrast to a fixed mindset, which assumes that your abilities are fixed and cannot be changed. When you have a growth mindset, you're more likely to see setbacks as opportunities to learn and grow, rather than as failures. This can help you stay motivated and focused on your goals, even when things get tough. I often find myself reminding my friends of a quote by Al Neuharth in these situations: "The difference between mountains and molehills is perspective."

With practice and commitment, these strategies and concepts can help you overcome setbacks and move forward with resilience and determination. By setting new goals, seeking new opportunities, practicing perseverance and resilience, and having a growth mindset, you can build the skills and mindset you need to succeed in any challenge that comes your way. Remember that setbacks are temporary, but your determination and resilience can last a lifetime.

While these things can help you face setbacks head-on, it's also important to have strong communication skills to boost your confidence and navigate difficult situations with ease. Effective communication skills can help you express your thoughts and feelings clearly, build strong relationships with others, and advocate for yourself in various settings. In the next chapter, we'll explore some key communication skills you can develop to boost your confidence and succeed in both personal and professional settings. Whether you're giving a presentation, having a difficult conversation with a friend or family member, or negotiating a job offer, these skills will help you communicate with confidence and clarity. So let's dive in and start building your communication toolkit!

MAIN POINTS

- Failure and rejection can feel like the end of the road, but they are actually opportunities to learn and grow.

- Some methods to cope with failure and rejection include mindfulness, self-compassion, and self-reflection.

- In order to bounce back from failure, it is important to set new goals, discover new opportunities, and maintain a growth mindset.

- Always remember that mistakes are not only okay, but are expected and (often) beneficial in the long run.

6.

FINDING YOUR VOICE:
BUILDING CONFIDENCE IN COMMUNICATION

"Communication - the human connection - is the key to personal and career success." -Paul J. Meyer

As a teenager, you're likely navigating a lot of new experiences and relationships. Whether it's with friends, family, or strangers, being able to communicate clearly and effectively is vital for making connections and achieving your goals. Communication isn't just about speaking and listening, though that certainly is an important facet of it. It's also about body language, tone of voice, delivery, and word choice. In this section, we'll explore why effective communication is so important, how it can affect self-confidence, and how to improve your own communication skills. I used to be the worst at communication, and these skills have helped me immensely.

I never gave much thought to how effective communication can boost self-confidence by helping you set boundaries with others.

When you can clearly communicate your needs and wants, you're less likely to feel like others are taking advantage of you or not respecting your wishes, which is an awful way to feel if you ask me. You should feel empowered in your interactions with others, not like a pushover.

Effective communication also helps you build positive relationships with others. When you can communicate your thoughts and feelings clearly and respectfully to others, they are more likely to understand where you're coming from and take you seriously. They will also see you as someone that will not stand for violation of your boundaries, so they will be less likely to even try. This can help you build trust and respect with others, which can further boost your own self-confidence. Let's not forget about problem-solving skills, either! When you can communicate effectively in your relationships, you're better able to work with others to find solutions to problems. This can help you feel more capable and confident in your abilities, which is a huge confidence booster, I tell you what.

EFFECTIVE COMMUNICATION: IT'S PERSONAL, NOT PERFECT

Learning how to communicate can be difficult and overwhelming without the proper skills in your self-improvement toolkit. There are plenty of resources that can tell you how to "properly" communicate, but the problem with them is that communication is very personal. There is no one right way to do it, which is why I prefer to use the term "effective." This helps emphasize that the most important thing is that your communication strategies work for you! With that being said, if you're finding it difficult to communicate effectively with your friends or family, don't worry - there are some techniques you can use to improve your communication skills.

Let's start with something called active listening. Active listening is all about showing the person you're talking to that you're really listening to what they're saying. This means focusing on the speaker, giving them your undivided attention, and responding in a way that shows you're engaged in the conversation. Here are some tips on how to actively listen:

- **Give the speaker your full attention:** This means putting away any distractions such as your phone, turning off the TV, or closing your laptop. It also means that you should not be thinking about what to have for dinner or whether you remembered to lock the door on the way out. People have a knack for knowing when they are being ignored, whether intentionally or not, and it is a horrible start if the person you are speaking to does not feel that they are important enough for your attention.

- **Make eye contact:** This shows the speaker that you're interested in what they're saying and that you're paying attention to them. Eye contact can feel intimidating or overwhelming for some people, so use your best judgment on how best to put this step to good use.

- **Ask questions:** Ask questions to clarify what the person means or to show that you're following along with the conversation. Many people tend to try to turn conversations around onto their own experiences, even without meaning to. It is important to give each person in a conversation the time to speak without interrupting or inserting your own thoughts unless prompted.

- **Use non-verbal cues:** Use non-verbal cues such as nodding your head or smiling to show that you're engaged in the conversation. This is an easy one, but it can go a long way. However, you shouldn't just smile and nod to placate your conversational partner. If you aren't listening, you could accidentally respond in a manner not appropriate for the conversation.

When you actively listen, you are not only hearing what the other person has to say, but you are understanding it. Nobody wants to feel like someone is only interested in what they can add to the conversation. By actively listening, you can ensure that your conversational partner feels valid and heard, which facilitates open and honest communication.

Another technique to consider is assertiveness training. Assertiveness is all about expressing your thoughts and feelings in a clear and confident way, while still being respectful of others. Assertiveness can be challenging, especially when you may be worried about fitting in or being liked by your peers. Here are some tips on how to be assertive:

- **Be clear:** Speak in a clear and concise manner. Make sure you express your thoughts and feelings in a way that's easy to understand. This can be hard to do in stressful situations, but it is very important for healthy and effective communication.

- **Use "I" statements:** Start your sentences with "I" to express your thoughts and feelings. For example, say "I feel" instead of "You make me feel". This alone has brought my conversational success rates up so far. It doesn't feel like you're blaming the other person, and it shows that you have the maturity to own your feelings as your own.

- **Be respectful:** Remember to be respectful of the other person's thoughts and feelings. Avoid attacking or blaming them for their opinions. Disrespectful comments are a prime way to end a conversation before it has even started, especially in tense situations.

- **Practice:** You should practice being assertive in low-pressure situations, such as with close friends or family members, before using these techniques in more challenging situations. It might feel kind of silly in the moment, but it is far more important to be prepared to communicate well than to save face and not ask for help when you need it.

I've had to remind a lot of people in my life that there is a big difference between being assertive and being mean. As long as you are respectful in your assertions, you can make yourself heard and understood while still validating your conversational partner's thoughts and feelings.

Considering how much communication hinges on it, it would be negligent to forget about the importance of body language and non-verbal communication. Non-verbal communication refers to body language, facial expressions, and tone of voice. It can greatly affect how your message is received, and can either support or detract from what you're saying. Here are some tips on how to use non-verbal communication effectively:

- **Make eye contact:** Making eye contact shows that you're interested in what the other person is saying and that you're engaged in the conversation.

- **Use open body language:** Open body language such as uncrossed arms or relaxed shoulders, shows that you're open to the other person's ideas and feelings.

- **Watch your tone of voice:** Your tone of voice can convey a lot about how you're feeling. Make sure you're speaking in a tone that supports your message.

- **Pay attention to facial expressions:** Your facial expressions can also convey a lot about how you're feeling. Make sure you're using appropriate facial expressions to support your message.

Though the number varies, many experts agree that anywhere from 70-90% of communication is nonverbal. That means that you can say more with your body than you are with your words sometimes, hence the importance of mastering utilizing and interpreting nonverbal signals and body language.

MASTERING REAL-LIFE COMMUNICATION: TECHNIQUES TO PRACTICE AND PERFECT

Now that you have some great communication techniques in your arsenal, it's time to start putting them into practice in real-life situations! I know you may be asking yourself where to start, especially if some of the things we discussed are new to you. So, let's explore some strategies for using communication skills in everyday scenarios.

One great way to practice your communication skills is through role playing. This means acting out different scenarios with a friend or family member, where you can practice your active listening, assertiveness, and non-verbal communication skills. I know it may feel kind of silly or embarrassing at first, but I promise you it really does help. I have role-played difficult conversations with my friends and family and it has helped me understand what is needed to convey what I want to without coming across as rude or upsetting the person I am talking to. If you're unsure where to start, here are a few examples that you can use to shape your own practice:

- **Expressing your feelings to a friend:** Let's say you're upset with a friend because they canceled plans last minute. You can role play the scenario with a family member or another friend, and practice expressing your feelings in a calm and respectful way. For example, you might say something like, "Hey, I was really looking forward to our plans, and I felt hurt when you canceled at the last minute. Can we talk about how we can make sure this doesn't happen again in the future?"

- **Asking for help:** Let's say you're struggling with a school assignment and need some help from your teacher. You can role play the scenario with a family member or friend, and practice asking for help in a clear and concise way. For example, you might say something like, "Hi, I'm having some trouble with this assignment and I was wondering if you could help me understand it better?"

- **Negotiating with a sibling:** Let's say you and your sibling are arguing over who gets to use the computer. You can role play the scenario with a parent or another family member, and practice using assertive communication to negotiate a solution. For example, you might say something like, "I understand that you want to use the computer, but I also need to use it for my homework. Can we come up with a schedule that works for both of us?"

By practicing these scenarios in a role play setting, you can become more comfortable with using effective communication techniques in real-life situations. After the role play, it's important to seek feedback from your partner. Ask them for their honest opinion on how you did, and what aspects you could improve on. Maybe your tone could use some work, or you worded things in a way that did not get your point across. Remember, feedback is a gift! So, take it in stride and use it to make improvements for next time. The goal of role playing is to practice your skills in a safe and supportive environment. Don't be afraid to make mistakes!

Another important aspect of communication is authenticity and clarity. Authenticity and clarity in self-expression relies on your ability to be honest with yourself and others about how you're feeling. You should be communicating your thoughts and feelings in a clear and concise manner, regardless of the situation. This can be particularly challenging for teenagers and some. adults, as there my be pressure to fit in with their peers or hide their true feelings. For example, let's say you're in a group conversation and someone makes a comment that you don't agree with. Instead of going along with what everyone else is saying, you can express your opinion in a clear and respectful way. This could mean saying something like, "I scc where you're coming from, but I actually have a different perspective on this topic." Of course, that's just an example. The important thing to remember is that by being authentic and expressing yourself clearly, you showing that you value your own opinions and feelings, and that you're willing to communicate them effectively. This can lead to stronger relationships and a greater sense of self-confidence.

Relationships and general happiness can be improved through development of communication skills. You can improve your communication skills and forge closer bonds with the people in your life by working on being assertive, practicing active listening, and remembering what you have learned about non-verbal communication. Despite all of this, it is crucial to keep in mind that leading a fulfilling life requires more than just sharp communication skills. In the next chapter, we'll explore some strategies for removing negative influences from your life and creating a more positive and supportive environment. By combining these strategies with your newly-acquired and sharpened communication skills from this chapter, you'll be well on your way to a happy, confident life.

MAIN POINTS

- Communication skills are learned, we are not born with them.

- Proper communication skills can improve confidence by helping you set and enforce healthy boundaries, build relationships, and improve your interpersonal problem-solving skills.

- It's not about perfect communication, but rather effective communication.

- Helpful communication techniques to practice include active listening, assertiveness training, and role-playing (with feedback).

- Nonverbal communication, authenticity, clarity, and active listening are the key ingredients in the recipe for effective communication.

7.

THE NEGATIVITY DETOX:
SAY GOODBYE TO THE BAD VIBES

"The less you respond to negative people, the more powerful your life will become." – Robert E. Baine, Jr.

Have you ever felt like negative or toxic aspects of your life are holding you back? Maybe it's a relationship that drains your energy, a job that makes you miserable, or a habit that you know is bad for you. We have all been there, in some way. Whatever the case may be, it can be difficult to break away from these negative influences and create a more positive and fulfilling life. However, identifying and removing them is a crucial step towards living a happier and more satisfying life. In this chapter, we'll explore why it's so important to remove negativity from your life, and some strategies you can use to do just that. By taking control of your environment and creating a more positive and supportive space, you'll be able to thrive and reach your full potential.

NAVIGATING SOCIAL MEDIA: THE GOOD, THE BAD, AND THE UGLY

Social media can be a fun and useful tool for staying connected with friends, sharing your life, and exploring new ideas. However, it's no secret that social media can also be a breeding ground for negativity and toxicity. As a teenager, you have a higher likelihood of being exposed to the positive and negative aspects of social media. While social media can have its ups (easy communication, entertainment, etc), it can also exacerbate insecurities by presenting an unrealistic and often idealized version of life that can be damaging to your confidence and self-esteem. It also allows for cyberbullying, which can be mentally and emotionally damaging.

One of the biggest ways social media can negatively impact your confidence is by promoting comparison. When you see other people's highlight reels on social media, it's easy to start feeling like your own life doesn't measure up. You might feel like you're not pretty enough, smart enough, or popular enough compared to the people you see online. This can lead to feelings of inadequacy and low self-worth. In addition to promoting comparison, social media can also be a breeding ground for misinformation and unrealistic expectations. Many influencers and celebrities use their platforms to promote an idealized and often unrealistic version of life, which can be damaging to your mental health. When you see someone promoting a perfect life, it's important to remember that what you see online is often not the full picture. People typically only post the highlights of their lives, and may not show the struggles and hardships that come with it.

If you find that social media is negatively impacting your mental health or self-esteem, it might be time to take a break. Here are some tips for reducing your social media use:

- **Set limits:** Try setting limits on how much time you spend on social media each day. It may be helpful to set a timer or use an app that tracks your usage. I personally have my TikTok account set up to remind me to take a break after 20 minutes of usage. I did this after realizing how easy it was to spend an hour or more straight scrolling through my feed. Oops.

- **Take breaks:** Consider taking regular breaks from social media, such as a week-long hiatus or a social media-free weekend. This can feel difficult at first, especially for people who have grown up with social media, but ideally you will be left feeling refreshed and grateful for your own life and what you have.

- **Curate your feed:** You have a great level of control over what you see on social media, minus the ads that tend to be thrown in your face by companies with nothing better to do. Consider unfollowing accounts that make you feel bad about yourself, and following accounts that promote positivity and self-love. I follow a ridiculous number of cute animals on social media because seeing them makes me happy. I am much happier with that than I was with constant negativity.

- **Find other ways to connect:** Remember that social media isn't the only way to connect with friends and family. Try reaching out to people in person or over the phone instead. When my friends and I go out to eat, we all put our phones in a pile. If someone looks at their phone (unless it's for an emergency) they pay for the meal. It does a great job of encouraging face-to-face communication and often leads to some hilarious conversations. I also call my mom weekly to catch up. I've gotten a lot closer with people since starting to rely less on social media for my communication.

By taking steps to reduce your social media use and curate your feed to promote positivity, you can protect your mental health and boost your confidence. Remember, social media can be a powerful tool, but it's important to use it in a way that supports your well-being.

DON'T FEED THE TROLLS: DEALING WITH CYBERBULLIES AND PROTECTING YOUR WELL-BEING

Unfortunately, the freedom and connectivity that makes social media so useful also makes it a perfect tool for cyberbullies. Cyberbullying is the use of technology to harass, intimidate, or humiliate someone. It can take many forms, such as spreading rumors, making hurtful comments, or sharing embarrassing photos or videos. The hardest part is that it can happen at any time, and the victim can't always escape it. The anonymity provided by many websites can make it difficult or impossible to find the person responsible, but it is still important to report instances of cyberbullying to a trusted adult. Due to the potential of serious consequences, including depression, anxiety, and even suicide, cyberbullying is illegal in a majority of U.S. states. If you experience cyberbullying, it's important to take action. Here are some steps you can take:

- **Take a break:** If cyberbullying is causing you significant distress, it may be time to take a break from social media or any online platforms that may be contributing to the problem. While it is not your fault, and you shouldn't have to leave the situation, sometimes the best option (at least short-term) is to avoid the negative messages and regain a sense of control.

- **Save evidence:** If you receive hurtful messages or comments, be sure to take screenshots or save the messages as evidence. This can be useful if you decide to report the cyberbullying to the relevant authorities or platform moderators.

- **Block the bully:** If you know who the person bullying you is, it is wise to block them on all social media and other online platforms. This will prevent them from continuing to harass you while you try to resolve the conflict.

- **Report the incident:** Most social media platforms have reporting tools that allow users to report cyberbullying. If you experience cyberbullying, use these tools to report the incident and provide any evidence you have collected.

- **Seek support:** Cyberbullying can be emotionally challenging and mentally exhausting. I recently had a random player on a video game get so mad about losing that he tried to insult my entire personality in personal messages after the game ended. Talk about a waste of everyone's time. When people treat you this way, it's important to seek support from friends, family members, or a mental health professional. They can provide a listening ear, offer advice, and help you develop coping strategies.

- **Take care of yourself:** Cyberbullying can take a massive toll on your mental and physical health, so it's important to prioritize self-care. Engaging in activities that make you feel good, such as exercise, hobbies, or spending time with friends, will contribute to lifting your spirits and making you feel valued.

No matter what anyone may say, I want you to know that cyberbullying is never okay. You don't deserve to be treated poorly, and it is never your fault. If you see someone else being cyberbullied, it's important to speak up and offer your support. Together, we can create a safer and more positive online environment, one person at a time. If you see someone else being cyberbullied, it's important to speak up and offer your support. Together, we can create a safer and more positive online environment, one person at a time.

WHEN SAYING GOODBYE IS NECESSARY: SIGNS OF A TOXIC RELATIONSHIP

This seems like a great time to segue into another very important topic in this chapter. We all have relationships that don't serve us well. It could be a friend who always puts you down, a partner who is emotionally abusive, or a family member who constantly criticizes you. These relationships can be toxic, draining, and have a negative impact on your mental health. Knowing when and how to say goodbye to toxic relationships is unbelievably important for your wellness and your self-confidence.

Toxic relationships can manifest in different ways, but they all have one thing in common: they make you feel bad about yourself. Whether it's through constant criticism, manipulation, or disrespect, these relationships can chip away at your self-esteem and leave you feeling depleted. It doesn't matter what your relationship to the person is, if they consistently make you feel worse about yourself, it may be worth reevaluating their place in your life. But before we get into that whole process, let's first talk about how to tell whether a relationship might not be as great for you as you thought it would be. Identifying toxic relationships is the first step towards ending them. Here are some signs that you may be in a toxic relationship:

- **Lack of respect:** In a toxic relationship, there is often a lack of respect and consideration for each other's feelings and boundaries. If your partner or friend is always putting you down, making fun of you, or belittling your thoughts and opinions, it's a sign of disrespect and a red flag.

- **Manipulation:** Toxic individuals may use manipulative tactics to control you or get their way. This can include guilt-tripping, gaslighting, or threatening to leave if you don't do what they want.

Gaslighting is a form of emotional abuse in which the abuser manipulates the victim to doubt their own perceptions, memories, and sanity. It's a tactic used to gain power and control over the victim by making them question their own reality. The abuser in a situation may deny that certain events occurred or distort the truth in a way that makes the victim doubt their own recollection of events. Over time, gaslighting can lead the victim to feel confused, anxious, and even question their own sanity. If you notice this behavior in any of your relationships, it is important to seek help.

- **Constant criticism:** If a partner or friend is always criticizing you and making you feel bad about yourself, that is a clear sign of a toxic relationship. It's important to be around someone who supports and encourages you, rather than tearing you down. We are past the point of telling others and ourselves that people are mean to us because they like us or are jealous. This was something that never should have been conceptualized to begin with. If someone cares, they will treat you right. People do not abuse others out of love.

- **Lack of trust:** If someone is constantly checking up on you when you are not together, accusing you of cheating, or invading your privacy, it's a sign of a toxic dynamic. Privacy is a right, not a sign of suspicious behavior.

- **Emotional abuse:** Emotional abuse can take many forms, including (but not limited to) name-calling, verbal attacks, or withholding affection as a form of punishment. If you're experiencing any form of emotional abuse in your relationship, it's important to seek help and get out of the situation. Your safety and wellbeing should be priority number one, be it mental or physical.

This seems like a good point for yet another story, so feel free to grab a snack. I once had a romantic partner who seemed absolutely perfect. We will call him Joe. Joe was kind, attentive, and seemed to really care about me... at first. We met at a mutual friend's party and hit it off immediately. We started texting and calling each other every day, and before long, we were spending all our free time together. At first, everything was great. We had so much in common, and I loved spending time with him. But over time, I began to notice some red flags in our relationship.

Joe would frequently cancel plans at the last minute, refuse to compromise on anything, and become angry and defensive when I tried to express my feelings or concerns. For example, one time we had made plans to go to a concert together. I was really looking forward to it, but on the day of the concert, he texted me saying that he had to work late and couldn't make it. I was disappointed, but I understood that work can be unpredictable, so I suggested that we make new plans on another day. Thing is, he didn't seem interested in rescheduling and just said that we'd "catch the next one."

He would cancel plans or be late without warning, and I found myself constantly waiting around for him. When I tried to talk about it, he would brush me off or get defensive, saying that I was overreacting or being too demanding. I found myself constantly walking on eggshells around him, afraid to say or do anything that might set them off. He would often give me the silent treatment or blame me for things that weren't my fault. I remember one time, I caught him going through my phone after coming out of the bathroom, only to be told that I shouldn't care unless I had something to hide.

At first, I tried to make excuses for Joe's behavior and convince myself that things would get better. I thought that maybe he was just going through a tough time, or that I was being too sensitive. But the more I tried to make things work, the worse it became. I realized that I was in a toxic relationship and that I needed to get out before it caused any more damage to my mental health and self-esteem. It was hard to end things, but I knew it was the right decision for me. I talked to a close friend about what was going on, and they helped me see that I deserved better. I ended things with Joe within a week of that conversation and took some time to focus on myself. I surrounded myself with friends who were supportive and encouraging, and slowly began to rebuild my confidence and sense of self-worth. I am glad that I am the person I am today, and I know that contributed to it, but it does not make that time in my life any less difficult to look back on.

If you recognize signs like the ones we have talked about so far in a relationship, it's important to take steps to protect yourself. Setting boundaries is one of the most effective strategies for dealing with toxic people. This ties into the previous chapter on communication skills. When you set boundaries, you communicate clearly what you are willing and not willing to accept from others. This can help you regain a sense of control and protect yourself from further harm. For example, if a friend is constantly putting you down, you could set a boundary by saying, "I don't appreciate it when you criticize me like that. If you can't speak to me respectfully, I don't want to spend time with you."

It's also important to surround yourself with positive influences. Your friends should bring you up, not bring you down. Being around people who inspire and support you can help boost your self-esteem and give you the courage to end toxic relationships. Ending a toxic relationship can be challenging, but it's always beneficial in the long run. Toxicity is never healthy, as much as we try to convince ourselves that it isn't "that bad." Here are some tips for ending a toxic relationship in a healthy way:

1. **Identify your reasons for ending the relationship:** Before ending a toxic relationship, you should identify exactly why you're doing it. This will help you stay firm in your decision and not second-guess yourself when it comes time to end things. Take some time to reflect on your relationship and write down your reasons for ending it. Remember this when communicating your wants and needs.

2. **Be clear and direct:** The best way to end a toxic relationship is to be honest and direct. Don't mince words or exaggerate or sugarcoat the situation. Simply state that you've decided to end the relationship because it isn't working for you. That is reason enough. I assure you.

3. **Set boundaries:** It's crucial to establish boundaries if the toxic person tries to get in touch with you after you've ended the relationship. Inform them of your need for solitude and your disinterest in continuing the relationship.

4. **Don't engage in arguments or blame games:** It's typical for the other person to become defensive, argumentative, or try to place the blame for the issues in the relationship when ending a toxic relationship.

Avoid arguments and blame-shifting. Just be clear about why you're ending the relationship and be steadfast in your decision.

5. **Seek support:** It's crucial to get support from friends, family, or a therapist when ending a toxic relationship because doing so can be emotionally taxing. You can process your feelings and feel less alone by sharing your experience with others.

6. **Focus on self-care:** After ending a toxic relationship, it's high time to focus on self-care. This may include engaging in activities that make you happy, practicing mindfulness or meditation, or seeking therapy. There's still a lot of stigma surrounding therapy, but boy oh boy does it help so much. Taking care of yourself will help you move on from the toxic relationship and start to heal.

HABITS THAT HELP, HABITS THAT HINDER: STRATEGIES FOR SUCCESS

Once you've dealt with external factors that seep negativity into your life, it's time to take a look inward again. We all have bad habits that we wish we could break. Maybe it's biting your nails, procrastinating, or spending too much time on your phone. While these habits might seem harmless, they can actually have a negative impact on your self-confidence. Bad habits can negatively impact your self-confidence in many ways. For example, if you have a habit of procrastination, you might feel stressed and overwhelmed when you don't meet deadlines, leading to a negative impact on your confidence. Similarly, if you have a habit of negative self-talk, you might start to believe those negative thoughts and feel unworthy or inadequate. By breaking these bad habits, you can improve your self-confidence and feel better about yourself.

The first step in breaking bad habits is to identify them. This can be done by self-reflection and awareness. Here are some tips for identifying bad habits:

- Be aware of your behavior: The first step in identifying bad habits is to pay attention to your behavior. Be mindful of your actions, thoughts, and emotions throughout the day. Take note of the things you do without thinking, or the habits you have that you're not proud of.

- Listen to feedback: Sometimes, we're not aware of our bad habits until someone else points them out. If someone you trust gives you feedback about a behavior that's negatively impacting them or you, listen and take note.

- Check your motivation: Consider why you engage in certain behaviors. Are you doing something because it's truly important to you, or because you feel like you should? Understanding your motivations can help you identify habits that aren't serving you.

- Reflect on your goals: Think about your short-term and long-term goals, and consider whether your habits are helping or hindering your progress. If a habit is standing in the way of your goals, it's likely a bad habit.

- Monitor your emotions: Pay attention to how you feel before, during, and after engaging in certain habits. If a habit leaves you feeling guilty, anxious, or ashamed, it's likely not a positive one.

Once you've identified your bad habits, you can start working on breaking them. Breaking habits is difficult, as they often become a part of you, but it is not impossible. There are certain steps you can take in the habit-breaking process that will lend to your success.

1. **Set a goal:** Decide what you want to achieve by breaking the habit. For example, if you want to cut back on phone usage, set a goal to decrease your usage by an hour. Once you have adjusted to the new limit, you can increase it in increments until you reach your end goal.

2. **Replace the bad habit with a good one:** Replace your bad habit with a healthy habit that can give you a similar sense of reward. For example, if you tend to eat junk food when you're stressed, try going for a walk instead. It is much easier to break a bad habit if you find something to replace the behavior with.

3. **Use positive reinforcement:** Reward yourself for breaking the habit. For example, if you go a week without checking social media during work hours, treat yourself to a movie or a nice dinner. Positive reinforcement works way better than being negative and harsh on yourself.

4. **Ask for support:** Ask your friends or family for support in breaking the habit. Having someone to hold you accountable can make a big difference.

5. **Keep track of your progress:** Keep a journal or a habit tracker to monitor your progress. You can use this to keep yourself motivated and to gauge your progress. Looking back on your journey and realizing how much you have achieved can be very satisfying.

Only half of the battle is won by breaking bad habits. It's crucial to establish fresh, constructive habits that will help you achieve your goals and boost your confidence. Here are some strategies for creating new, positive habits:

1. **Start small:** Focus on one habit at a time and start small. For example, if you want to start exercising, start with a 10-minute walk each day. Once this is routine, you can start walking for 20 minutes each day. Then maybe you can start doing body-weight exercises a few times a week. You can increase and alter your goals as you form new habits.

2. **Make it easy:** Make developing new habits as simple as possible. For instance, if you want to read more, try leaving a book on your nightstand and read some before bed every night. I've found this particular method works well with a variety of habits. A three-step task is far easier to accept and work on than a five or ten-step task. By simplifying the process, you are making it as easy to succeed as you can.

3. **Be consistent:** Consistency is the key to creating a new habit. Try to do it at the same time every day or every week. This is especially important with habits like remembering to take medication.

4. **Use positive reinforcement:** Reward yourself for practicing the new habit. For example, if you exercise three times a week for a month, treat yourself to a massage. You've earned it!

In this chapter, we talked about how removing unfavorable people and situations from your life can improve your mental and emotional well-being. We discussed techniques for establishing boundaries with toxic people, quitting bad habits, and lessening the detrimental effects of social media on your self-esteem. Building and upholding healthy relationships and habits requires being true to yourself and surrounded by positive influences.

In the next chapter, we'll delve deeper into the topic of self-confidence, exploring ways to maintain and improve it on a daily basis. By continuing to prioritize your mental and emotional wellbeing, you'll be better equipped to navigate life's challenges and pursue your dreams with confidence and resilience.

MAIN POINTS

- Purging toxic aspects of your life is vital for your long-term health and happiness.

- Social media can have its ups and downs, and it is important to have a healthy relationship with it.

- Cyberbullying is an unfortunately common issue that nobody should have to deal with. Do not hesitate to seek help if you or someone you know is a victim of cyberbullying.

- Be aware of the indicators of a toxic relationship:
    - Lack of respect
    - Manipulation
    - Constant criticism
    - Lack of trust
    - Emotional abuse

- When cutting a toxic person from your life, it is important to do the following:
    - Identify the reason that you are leaving, and remember it if you ever have doubts.
    - Be clear and direct about what you want and why.
    - Set boundaries and stick to them.
    - Do not engage in arguments and blame games.
    - Take good care of yourself and seek support from your loved ones, friends, and any other consistent people capable of being there for you.
- Building good habits is just as important for living your best life as breaking bad ones.

8.

KEEPING THE MOMENTUM:

MAINTENANCE AND CONSISTENCY IN CONFIDENCE BUILDING

"I am the measure of my worth, and I say I am worthy."
- Unknown

Have you ever found yourself feeling unsure of yourself, maybe even doubting your abilities or feeling a bit lost? It's totally normal to go through ups and downs when it comes to self-confidence, especially during these wild teenage years. But the good news is that there are practical ways to build and maintain your self-confidence, and that's what we're going to explore in this chapter. We'll talk about why maintaining self-confidence is so important, how to create a positive and supportive environment for self-improvement, and some killer strategies for staying motivated and focused on personal growth. Whether you're dealing with social anxiety, academic stress, or just trying to figure out what you want in life, cultivating self-confidence can be a game-changer. So, let's dive in and discover how you can level up your self-esteem and crush your goals like a boss!

Now that we've introduced the topic, let's dive into why maintaining and improving self-confidence is so critical, particularly during the teenage years. Self-confidence can be defined as a belief in one's abilities, qualities, and judgment. When you have high self-confidence, you're more likely to take risks, try new things, and handle setbacks without losing your footing. On the other hand, low self-confidence can hold you back, make you second-guess yourself, and prevent you from reaching your full potential. That's why it's crucial to maintain and improve your self-confidence over time, especially during your teenage years when you're still figuring out who you are and what you want in life.

But let's be real: maintaining self-confidence as a teenager can be incredibly difficult. You're going through a lot of changes, both physically and emotionally, and you're also dealing with social pressures, academic stress, and personal identity issues. For instance, you might feel that you must fit in with a particular group of people or look a certain way to be accepted, or you might be having trouble in school and believe that you are not smart enough. Not to mention body image; given all the pressure to look a certain way, it is understandable why so many teenagers struggle with self-confidence.

What can you do, then, to overcome these obstacles and keep your confidence? We'll look at some useful strategies and techniques in more detail in the section after this. But first, let's pause for a moment to remind ourselves that you're not alone in this; it's completely normal for teenagers to experience some degree of self-confidence issues. The fact that you're starting to work on it is what matters most!

MOTIVATION AND FOCUS: STAYING ON TRACK TOWARDS PERSONAL GROWTH

Maintaining and improving self-confidence requires more than just positive thinking and believing in yourself. It also requires taking action and making intentional choices that help you grow as a person. Here are some strategies that can help you stay motivated and focused on your personal growth journey:

1. **Set and pursue new goals:** Setting goals is a great way to stay motivated and focused on your personal growth. When you have a clear target in mind, it's easier to stay on track and measure your progress. Plus, achieving goals can give you a sense of accomplishment and boost your self-confidence. So, think about what you want to achieve in different

areas of your life – such as academics, sports, hobbies, or personal relationships – and set realistic, specific goals to work towards.

2. **Engage in self-reflection and seek feedback from others:** Self-reflection is another powerful tool for personal growth. Take some time to reflect on your strengths, weaknesses, values, and goals, and think about how you can improve in different areas. It's also important to seek feedback from others, such as teachers, coaches, friends, or family members. Ask them for constructive criticism and listen to their suggestions – it can help you gain a new perspective and improve your skills.

3. **Challenge yourself and seek new experiences:** Finally, don't be afraid to step outside your comfort zone and try new things. Challenging yourself and seeking new experiences can help you grow as a person, build resilience, and increase your self-confidence. Whether it's trying a new hobby, taking on a leadership role, or traveling to a new place, embrace opportunities for growth and don't let fear hold you back.

Setting and pursuing new goals is an important aspect of personal growth and self-confidence. When you set goals, you give yourself something to work towards and it can help you stay motivated and focused. Clarifying your priorities and values is one advantage of goal-setting. You can make deliberate decisions that are in line with your values and priorities by reflecting on the goals you have for various aspects of your life.

Setting goals also enables you to track your development and recognize your accomplishments along the way, which is a benefit. You can see how far you've come and be proud of your accomplishments when you have a clear goal to work toward. This may inspire you to continue by acting as a confidence booster.

To achieve your goals, you frequently need to push yourself outside of your comfort zone, acquire new skills, and deal with obstacles. You may feel more competent and convinced of your skills and abilities as a result. As you develop new skills and overcome challenges, you'll gain a sense of accomplishment and pride in yourself, which can contribute to your overall self-confidence.

STEPPING OUTSIDE YOUR COMFORT ZONE: CHALLENGING YOURSELF FOR GROWTH

Self-reflection and seeking feedback from others are important tools for personal growth and can help you maintain and improve your self-confidence over time. Self-reflection involves taking time to think about your thoughts, feelings, and behaviors, and how they impact your life. By examining yourself in this way, you can gain insight into your strengths and weaknesses, and identify areas where you can improve.

In addition to self-reflection, seeking feedback from others can also be helpful. It can be difficult to see ourselves objectively, and others may be able to provide us with valuable insights that we may not have considered otherwise. Receiving constructive feedback can help us identify areas where we need to improve, and help us develop a plan to address those areas.

It's critical to surround yourself with people you respect, trust, and who genuinely care about you when asking for feedback. Furthermore, it's essential to approach criticism with an open mind and a desire to get better. Although receiving criticism can be painful, it's important to keep in mind that constructive criticism aims to improve you rather than diminish you.

One more key strategy for self-improvement and personal growth is to keep pushing yourself and seek out diverse experiences. We nudge ourselves to grow and learn new abilities when we venture outside of our comfort zones and embrace new challenges. Our ego and willingness to face new challenges can both increase as a result of this. We can build resilience and a growth mindset by putting ourselves through challenges. Resilience refers to our ability to rebound from setbacks. A growth mindset is the conviction that our skills and intelligence can be improved with effort and commitment. By taking on new challenges and pushing ourselves outside our comfort zones, we can develop these qualities and become more resilient and growth-oriented individuals.

Let's discuss the significance of pushing yourself and seeking out novel experiences. You know that sense of pride and accomplishment you have when you master a new skill or accomplish something you never thought you could? Challenge yourself, and sometimes magic happens. You push yourself outside of your comfort zone and into unfamiliar territory when you push yourself and try new things. Although this can seem distressing, it is also intriguing because it presents fresh chances for development and learning. There are countless opportunities for broadening your horizons and discovering new passions, whether it be by taking up a new hobby, learning a foreign language, or giving back to your neighborhood.

You can build resilience and adaptability by continuing to challenge yourself. When you encounter challenges or setbacks, you learn how to navigate past them and keep moving forward. This increases your self-efficacy and confidence in your capability to handle any situation. Additionally, it aids in the development of a growth mindset, in which difficulties and failures are viewed as chances for development. So, don't be afraid to experiment and leave your comfort zone. You'll be surprised at how much you can learn and develop if you look for new experiences that are exciting and challenging.

THE POWER OF POSITIVITY: HOW A SUPPORTIVE ENVIRONMENT CAN HELP YOU ACHIEVE YOUR GOALS

You can develop your self-confidence and move closer to your goals by pushing yourself and looking for new experiences. You don't have to do it alone, though, so keep that in mind. For long-term maintenance and growth of your self-confidence, it is essential to cultivate a positive and encouraging environment. When you surround yourself with people who uplift and encourage you, it becomes much easier to believe in yourself and your abilities. In this section, we'll explore some strategies you can use to cultivate such an environment, including seeking out positive role models and mentors, surrounding yourself with supportive friends and family, and more. So let's dive in!

To preserve and improve your self-esteem, you must create a favorable and encouraging environment for ongoing personal growth. Maintaining a positive and encouraging social environment is one of the most crucial tactics. You can have a big impact on how you feel about yourself by selecting the people you want to spend time with. Go out of your way to find friends and family who will help you feel good about yourself and who will support your dreams and goals. As you strive to boost your self-confidence, these individuals can provide you with inspiration, motivation, and advice. You can also look for groups of individuals who have similar interests and values to you. Connecting in this way can help you find people who support and understand your quest for greater self-assurance.

Searching for mentors and positive role models is one more tactic for fostering a welcoming and encouraging environment. Having mentors and positive role models in your life can do wonders for your confidence. Positive role models can show others how to handle challenging circumstances, get over obstacles, and succeed. They can provide direction, encouragement, and inspiration as you strive to boost your self-assurance and achieve your objectives. For teenagers who are still figuring out who they are and what they want to do with their lives, having a mentor can also be incredibly beneficial. A mentor can provide individualized guidance and support based on their own knowledge and experiences, assisting you in overcoming obstacles and choosing the best course of action for your future.Positive role models and mentors can offer guidance, inspiration, and encouragement as you work to improve your self-confidence. Look for people who have qualities or achievements that you admire, and consider asking them for advice or mentorship. Having someone to look up to and learn from can be a powerful motivator and help you stay on track towards your goals.

On a similar note, surrounding yourself with positive and supportive friends and family can also have a significant impact on your self-confidence. These individuals can offer encouragement, validation, and a listening ear when you need it most. They can also provide constructive feedback and support as you work towards your goals and pursue personal growth. Research has shown that social support is strongly linked to self-esteem and self-confidence. When you have a network of positive and supportive people in your life, you're more likely to feel confident in your abilities, take risks, and pursue your passions.

In addition to seeking out positive people and role models, it's important to practice self-compassion. When things don't go as planned, it's simple to be hard on yourself, but cultivating self-compassion entails treating yourself with the same respect and tolerance that you would extend to a close friend. Focus on growing from mistakes and failures rather than beating yourself up for them. Keep in mind that everyone makes mistakes and that it's acceptable to request assistance or support when necessary.

Last but not least, concentrate on constructing a physical environment that exudes warmth, welcome, and support. Adding inspiring and motivating items, like posters, photos, or quotes, to your bedroom, study space, or workspace can have a significant impact on how you feel about yourself and your surroundings. As you work toward your objectives, having a physical environment that feels empowering and encouraging can help you maintain focus and motivation. With these techniques in place, you can create a welcoming environment that encourages ongoing confidence growth.

Your personal development and self-confidence can advance significantly when you take the time to consider your accomplishments and strengths, make new goals, and challenge yourself. Although progress requires effort and tenacity, remember that it's not always easy. Create a supportive physical environment, surround yourself with uplifting and encouraging individuals, and look for constructive criticism. Remember to treat yourself well along the way as well! You can gradually boost your self-confidence by utilizing these techniques. Never forget that confidence is a powerful tool that can enable you to overcome obstacles, take calculated risks, and realize your objectives.

MAIN POINTS

- Starting this process is one thing; keeping it up and being consistent is quite another.

- Always push yourself to improve, but don't forget to acknowledge and celebrate your progress along the way.

- Seek out new experiences when possible. They will help you grow and expand your horizons.

- Try to cultivate a positive, supportive environment for yourself. Making your own cozy space in the physical world can be helpful on your journey of personal growth and development.

- Practice self-compassion daily. Although this process takes a lifetime, it is totally worthwhile and the benefits last a lifetime as well.

CONCLUSION

Congratulations! You've reached the conclusion of our confidence-building guide for teens. As you've probably realized by this stage, confidence is an ability that may be acquired and formed with repetition. Building self-confidence requires time and effort, but the rewards are all well worth it. You can harness the power of self-confidence and use it to start realizing your dreams by placing an emphasis on self-love, constructive self-talk, healthy boundaries, purpose, resilience, communication, and support. After working through the previous chapters, you should have a better understanding of how to cultivate your self-confidence, overcome negative thoughts, and develop the communication skills and self-love necessary to navigate life's challenges with ease.

I want to quickly circle back to something we talked about way back in the introduction. I hope you can see now that self-confidence truly is a superpower. It can help you overcome obstacles, achieve your goals, build healthy relationships, and live a life full of happiness and fulfillment - a life that you absolutely love. Many people chase this way of living for their whole lives, not realizing that the key to unlocking happiness starts with self-love. So embrace your unique qualities, celebrate your strengths, and always remember that you are worthy of love, respect, and success.

Like honing any superpower, building self-confidence is not always easy, and it can be challenging to maintain in the face of obstacles and setbacks. Some days you'll feel like you're on top of the world, and other days you'll feel like you're back at square one. That's okay. What's important is that you keep moving forward, keep practicing, and keep believing in yourself. Every failure and rejection is an opportunity to learn and grow. When things seem like they aren't going your way, gently remind yourself that self-confidence is not about being perfect or never experiencing failure. It's about believing in yourself and your ability to overcome challenges and achieve your goals, even when things get tough.

The good news is, with the strategies and techniques outlined in this book, you can continue to strengthen and improve your self-confidence throughout your life no matter what difficulties lay ahead. When you face challenges with a growth mindset, you'll be able to bounce back stronger and more resilient than ever before. It's important to remember that self-confidence is not a destination but a lifelong journey. It's something that you can continue to work on and improve throughout your life. So be kind to yourself and remember to practice self-care, self-compassion, and self-love every step of the way.

Let's revisit the significance of self-love and self-acceptance now that we've reviewed why confidence and the appropriate mindset matter. It's critical to accept your flaws and strengths, as well as to be kind to and compassionate toward yourself. You'll discover that you have the self-assurance to pursue your dreams and overcome any challenges that come your way when you love and accept yourself for who you are. I want you to stop, breathe, and consider what you learned from this experience when you find yourself having unfavorable thoughts about yourself or your surroundings. You must treat yourself with respect because you are the most significant person in your life. Nobody else will ever know you like the person reading these words right now, so show the world how great you are and how you deserve to be treated. Lead by example. Love yourself, and the rest will slowly start to fall into place.

Another important aspect of self-confidence is setting healthy boundaries. It's essential to know your limits and to communicate them clearly and assertively. This can help you avoid burnout, build strong relationships, and maintain your sense of self-worth. As we discussed just a moment ago, you lead the charge in establishing how you will be treated. If someone does not treat you with respect, compassion, and understanding, then it is okay to reevaluate their place in your life. Standing your ground against mistreatment by others is not mean, it is as necessary to a happy life as the air you breathe.

With that all covered, let's talk about one last core concept that will heavily impact your happiness and confidence. Discovering your purpose and pursuing your passions can be a transformative experience that not only brings you joy and fulfillment, but also helps to build your self-confidence. Taking part in activities that you are passionate about can give you a sense of direction, meaning, and purpose—all of which are crucial elements of a fulfilling life. Your sense of self and identity can be strengthened when you actively pursue your passions because you are living in accordance with your values and priorities.

Additionally, pursuing your passions can assist you in discovering and honing valuable talents and skills. The more you do things you like, the more skilled and proficient you'll naturally become at them, which can give you a sense of mastery and accomplishment. As you become more aware of your own abilities and potential, this can help to increase your self-confidence and self-esteem. Moreover, when you're pursuing your passions, you're often surrounded by like-minded individuals who share your interests and values. This can provide you with a sense of community and belonging, which can be a powerful source of support and encouragement. Being part of a community that values and celebrates your passions and accomplishments can help to reinforce your own sense of worth and self-confidence. This is all to say, find what you love, do it, and be proud. You'll thank yourself for it later.

I know we have reviewed a lot in this conclusion and covered even more in the previous chapters, so let me say one final thing. Thank you for taking the time to read this book on teenage confidence - you should be proud of yourself. I hope you found it helpful, informative, and inspiring. You are capable of achieving anything you set your mind to. I also hope that you feel empowered to continue cultivating your self-confidence and embracing the superpower that is within you. Don't forget to acknowledge and appreciate your accomplishments as you move forward on your path to greater confidence. You demonstrate your development and strength with each action you take, every objective you meet, and every boundary you establish. Therefore, take the time to acknowledge and appreciate your progress and use it as fuel to keep moving forward. Keep shining your light bright and never stop believing in yourself!

Made in the USA
Monee, IL
12 July 2023

39014295R00080